# THE DIARY OF JOSHUA WHITING
## FROM 1861 TO 1873

Joshua and Rebecca Whiting

# The Diary
# of Joshua Whiting
## (1820-1909)
of Hitchin, Hertfordshire
From 1861 to 1873
Citizen, Countryman and Quaker

*Compiled by*
Sarah Graham

William Sessions Limited
York, England

ISBN 1 85072 318 4

# Key

† indicates that there is further information
about the person in the Biographical section
which begins on page 76.

Numbered notes begin on page 103.

Printed in Palatino Typeface
from Author's Disk
by Sessions of York
The Ebor Press
York, England

# *Dedication*

Dedicated with affection and gratitude to the memory of
Reginald Leslie Hine and Mary Sturge Whiting.


*"It is a quiet backwater of life which the historian must inhabit
if he is to listen intently to the voices of the past."*
                                                                    *R. L. H.*

# Notes on illustrations

The photographs known to have been taken by Thomas B. Latchmore are those of Joshua and Rebecca Whiting (frontispiece), Thomas Whiting (page xiv), Joshua Whiting at Barclays Bank (page viii) and Scott of Steppingley (page 31).

The flower motifs throughout the book, at the beginning of each year, are taken from *The Children's Garden* by Agnes and Mary Catlow (1865) and were the work of Mrs Henry Criddle.

The two Samuel Lucas autotypes (page 29) were among a selection published by his brother Francis in 1890, including the latter's *Sketches of Rural Life and other Poems*. His sketches on pages 8, 14, 22, 43, 66, 67 and 70 are from the collection held by Hitchin Museum. Three paintings from the same collection appear in the colour section on pages 6, 7 and 8.

The cover of Samuel Bagster's book, *The Management of Bees* (1838), is shown on page 6 and the frontispiece (of bees) is on page 3 of the colour section.

The drawing on page 19 is the frontispiece from L.L. Langstroth's *A Practical Treatise on the Hive and Honeybee* (New York, 1860) and the illustration from the title page is on page xii.

The map of mid-nineteenth century Hitchin on pages xxii & xxiii was specially drawn for this book by Carola Scupham.

The map on page 1 of the colour section, captioned 'Road and Rail, the Bedfordshire Connection', was published by G.F. Cruchley, c. 1892, superimposed on a map of 1790. I am indebted to the Local Studies Library of Bedford Central Library for permission to use this map.

'19th Century Hitchin before the growth of suburbs', page 2 of colour section is the '1852 – Hitchin Local Board of Health Ordnance Map of the Town and Township of Hitchin'. The image of the map is reproduced by courtesy of Hertfordshire Archives and Local Studies.

'Furze Blossom with Mason or Lapidary Bee' and 'Wild Strawberry' on colour section pages 4 and 5 come from *Beauty in Common Things* (SPCK, n.d., c. 1890) illustrated by Mrs J. W. Whymper.

# Acknowledgments

There are a great many thanks to be recorded, quite apart from those given in the Introduction. It has been a continuing pleasure to work in a wide variety of libraries and museums, locally in Hitchin (first and foremost), Letchworth, Hertford (Hertfordshire Archives and Local Studies – HALS), Bedford and Ampthill, and in London, the London Metropolitan Archives, the Museum of Garden History and, vitally, the Library at Friends House, where the Diary itself will be deposited. I have had peaceful days of reading and writing at Woodbrooke Quaker Study Centre and at St Cuthman's, Coolham, and would like to thank the staff of all those establishments and communities for their friendly cooperation. On visits to the Library at Friends House over several years it has been a great help and pleasure to stay at the Penn Club.

I thank Barclays Group Archives in Manchester for their generous help and interest, Mssrs Shilcock in Hitchin for their readiness to assist in research on Spring Cottage, Bedford Road, and Messrs A&C Black for their permission to quote from the 1868 and 2005 editions of *Whitaker's Almanack*. Not only have I had a real sense of support from far-away friends and family, but I have been able to tap into the store of local knowledge held by friends in Hitchin, many being members of the Hitchin Historical Society and the Hitchin British Schools Trust. My warm thanks to them all.

I thank Eastway Enterprises for tackling my handwriting and Trish Carn for her expertise and the spur she has given me in the last stages of preparation. Since writing my initial round of thanks in the Introduction, the circle of support from the bee-keeping world has been enlarged by the interest of Tim Walton, advisor and correspondent to Dunton Community Garden, and Jeremy Burbage, of Northern Bee Books, to whom I am indebted for the inclusion of two precious illustrations from books in his collection. I thank Terry Hart for his invaluable *Quaker Chronology* and for his generosity in making those pages so widely accessible. From start to finish I have had the help and interest of William Sessions, Bob Sissons and Bob Jarrett of the Ebor Press and thank them warmly for their continual guidance and patience. Long friendship enabled me to call on the support and advice of Edward Milligan, Quaker historian extraordinary, and one-time librarian of the Library at Friends House. His enjoyment and understanding of the Diary have been an unfailing encouragement.

**Joshua Whiting leaving Barclays Bank**

# Introduction

The diary of Joshua Whiting, banker's clerk, covers the years 1861-1873. It has survived by chance and I am hopeful that this may prove a rewarding chance for a varied group of readers. Its first attraction for me is simply in the family link with the writer, my great-great uncle, but that receded as I began to realise that this is a rich document for Quakers, for Hitchin residents, gardeners, bankers and bee-keepers, and indeed for anyone interested in how a quiet life was lived in unquiet times.

I am writing this from my house in Hitchin, the Hertfordshire market town where I have lived for the last few years. I can just remember from childhood a framed photograph of him as an old man, stepping out of the bank, now Barclays, where he worked as a clerk for forty-four years. Prominent in the short High Street and only a few yards away from the house in Market Square where Joshua was born, the building is outwardly little changed. The photographer, his nephew Thomas Benwell Latchmore, had caught something in his bearing, both dignified and modest, which was very attractive. I had heard family elders talk of Uncle Joshua with real affection. There are other photographs with a suggestion of a family look and in his diary I sometimes catch a family turn of phrase, a coded aside, a reticence. There is nothing surprising about this sense of recognition, for we come of the same once closely guarded stock, the peculiarly close company of 'birthright' Friends, who as offspring of practising Quaker parents were (until 1959) entitled at birth to full membership of the Religious Society of Friends. Some explanation of the structure and practices of the mid-nineteenth century Quaker world and reminders of our continuing beliefs will be found in the accompanying notes in which I also hope to fill out and illuminate the local scene and suggest something of a world beyond Hitchin.

At this point I want to make sure of thanking all those who have ensured the survival of the diary, before going into a brief account of Joshua and his wife Rebecca. I am increasingly grateful to my cousin Richard Whiting for having entrusted me with the diary. We are all indebted to the old firm of Hitchin auctioneers, George Jackson's,† (sadly now no more) who, in the 1980s, took the trouble to trace Richard, himself never a Hitchin man, and alert him to a forthcoming sale of Whiting documents and photographs. These had belonged to Cousin Walter Whiting of Newlands Lane, one-time manager of the bank (Barclays since 1896) where Joshua, his great-uncle, had worked. Richard made a successful bid for these and ensured that they reached appropriate homes. Some years later I came to live in Hitchin and we had a cousinly reunion, identifying the sites, if not the actual buildings, of family homes, comparing the Meeting Houses, wondering and gossiping about our families and forebears. Thomas Shillitoe, once of Highbury, still stands out, apart, in our family history, a much loved, highly eccentric and inspirational figure, never to be forgotten. Richard realised how much at home I was feeling in Hitchin, and I thank him warmly for having given me the diary with the freedom to decide on its future as I thought best.

Since then there have been many setbacks and interruptions, but never a break in my certainty that this small, cloth-bound exercise book, its pages crammed with spidery jottings, observations, domestic details, comings and goings, notes and lists covering weather, flowers, birds, fruit and vegetables, family members, fellow-citizens and, just audible, an undercurrent of bees – all this makes up a very special heirloom. I was sure that this record, rich in the writer's enjoyment of the world around him and in his involvement with people, should be made available (and intelligible) for readers beyond the family circle.

The next round of thanks goes to Helen Osborn, for the professional transcription of the diary and for her interest in the project. She carried out meticulously the job I shirked and I am very grateful.

Lastly, my thanks to the enduring Quaker network of support. I was all but defeated by my ignorance about bees and all their ways when William Sessions, Quaker publisher, contacted David Gray,

Quaker bee-keeper, for guidance on my behalf. David enlisted Will Messenger, for not only is he another Quaker bee-keeper, but he is well-known as a historian in the bee-keeping world. His enthusiasm and understanding of the life and times of the Whitings has been a great encouragement, and his insight into Joshua's bee-keeping experience as well as explanations are a rich addition to the Notes. Thank you all.

I have taken my chief exercise to be in finding the right point at which to add the fleshing out of a name, the explanation of a term, something more of the townscape of Victorian Hitchin and help with the intricacies of Quaker practice. I do hope there may be readers interested in filling in some of the blanks and solving some of the puzzles for their own pleasure and satisfaction. Though I have tried not to disturb the casual nature of the diary, punctuation has often had to be amended for the sake of clarity. The text has been freed of the unfamiliar style of Quaker dating, and because I found 'Re' a very awkward abbreviation, Joshua's wife (when she's not 'the Lady' or 'R' has become Rebecca throughout.

I am very conscious of much being unfinished, some topics scarcely touched on, some not followed up at all, some unresolved. Every reader is likely to find something that they wish I'd handled differently. Family members may disagree among themselves, those who know Hitchin really well may be uneasy with some comments and Quaker historians may find good reason for criticism. I don't think this should worry me for it is the Diary that matters not the Notes. My only serious regret would be if I had in any way misunderstood or obscured the message of Joshua's notes, but I have real confidence that with so many good friends and advisors, I have not gone very far off course.

Three years ago I was writing from my Hitchin home in Tilehouse Street and now, in 2006, I'm still writing from Hitchin but from a few hundred yards away, in a new retirement flat in Whitings Court, appropriately named because the block covers a long stretch of ground approximating to the Whitings' Yard of the mid nineteenth century. I feel very lucky in having come to Hitchin late in life and being given this chance of coming so strangely close to a family of forebears.

**Sarah Graham**
**July 2006**

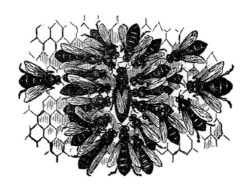

# Notes on Bee-keeping in the Diary of Joshua Whiting

Joshua Whiting was born on 10th September 1820 and tells us that his father was familiar with bee-keeping. We do not know when father or son commenced bee-keeping. It may well be that the family had maintained bees alongside other means of food production without seeing themselves as beekeepers as such. The diary starts on 16th October 1861, but the entry for 12th March 1868 refers to earlier records, giving dates that suggest that Joshua had been keeping bees since the late eighteen forties.

The period covered by his record is significant in bee-keeping history. The first entry, for 9th April 1854, is three years after the Great Exhibition in the Crystal Palace at Hyde Park when bees, beehives, and bee-keeping appliances were shown. The last entry, for 12th May 1873, is days after the publication of Number 1 of Volume 1 of *The British Bee Journal and Bee Keeper's Adviser* conducted by Charles Nash Abbott, Bee Master, of Hanwell, West London. In his introduction Abbott said "we do not anticipate much sympathy or support from the general public, nor can we hope to induce the bee-keeping cottager (so called) to abandon at once the superstitions and obscure theories by which that class of bee-keepers has been governed for so many generations. Our mission is to aid those enlightened members of the community who cultivate bees, and to induce others to engage in the charming pursuit, feeling assured that there is no other source of profit or amusement which affords such pleasant occupation, or yields so large a return for the capital invested when rightly understood and practised".

That introductory article also referred to a proposed Bee Guild whose purpose was "the advancement and improvement of the whole science of apiculture by the establishment of local clubs or conventions subject to a central authority". A year later this initiative led to the formation of the British Bee-Keepers' Association. The inaugural meeting took place on Saturday, 16th May 1874. These founding members had contributed to the Prize Fund of the Crystal Palace Bee and Honey Show which had been arranged to coincide with the Autumn Fruit and Flower Show taking place on the 8th, 9th and 10th September 1874. This was the first National Honey Show of the BBKA.

Joshua's diary records intelligent observation by a clearly capable man. He shows a keen interest in developing his bee-keeping, although in this he seems to be guided by his brother Thomas in Sheffield and his brother-in-law, Thomas Latchmore in Hitchin. Whether Joshua relied on others owing to their superior knowledge or skill, or simply used his obvious financial security to buy what others had made, is not entirely clear. As would be expected from someone in banking, Joshua pays attention to the cash realised from sale of honey, although it is clear that he was not dependent on this for his livelihood, but was using his resources more for the benefit of others; in 1863 Rebecca *gave* the town missionary a swarmed hive, and three years later they bought a hive back.

1869 was not a good honey season for Joshua. We can only speculate about why the entries about bees diminish from this point. Did the move to the new house during the winter of 1869/70 make bee-keeping less easy? Did the loss of Thomas Latchmore as a neighbour play a part? Was age taking its toll of their earlier enthusiasm? Since 1874, bee-keepers have had the benefit of organisation through the British Bee-Keepers' Association and latterly several other organisations. By placing Joshua's record in the context of the day, we see a man bridging the old village-based "cottager" rural economy and the modern science-based apiculture with which we are familiar today.

**Will Messenger, 2005**

## Two of Joshua's brothers in later life with John's wife and elder daughter

John Whiting

Anna Rebecca Whiting

Thomas Whiting

Anna Maria Whiting

# A lead into the Whiting family of Hitchin and the Society of Friends

I believe this is the right time to be valuing the record of a truly modest and very lovable man whose diary reflects the life of a certain time (the 1860s), a certain town (Hitchin) and a certain religious faith (Quakerism). Joshua worked for over forty years as banker's clerk for Sharples, Tuke and Co (to become Barclays in 1896). His great delight was in his gardens and his bees and in the surrounding countryside. In his marriage to Rebecca Jackson, he shared a rich life of friendships, domestic pleasures and anxieties, duties, obligations, 'outings', holidays and quietly held convictions. All this against the background of a steady job, the to's and fro's of family hospitality and a lively interest in other people and their work – and the hum of bees. The setting for a good life is outlined and there is much in the diary that unwittingly gives the reader a picture of the Whitings as very good Christians but, never, as Celia wonderfully described her sister Dorothea in *Middlemarch*, "too religious for family comfort". His notes suggest a warm homeliness and a readiness for enjoyment that offset the Whitings' steady attention to good works in the town, to the needs of their families and friends and to the demands of their Religious Society.

John and Margaret Whiting, Joshua's parents, were Quakers, living in the Market Square, hard by a slaughterhouse (John was a tanner and fellmonger), a stone's throw from the parish church, St Mary's, and two minutes walk from the River Hiz and the stench of sewage. Across the river was the no-go area of Dead Street (now Queen Street) with its filthy and overcrowded alleyways and yards. Three minutes walk in another direction was the Priory and its beautiful Park through which the Hiz ran clear and unpolluted. Behind the Whitings' house was a busy yard and behind that their garden and orchard. Around the Square were businesses and shops of all kinds and next to the Whiting house the Corn Exchange was built (1853) and down Cock Street (now High Street) the Bank (1845) in which Joshua was to spend all his working life. Beyond lay Bancroft, a wide street of handsome houses, some with gardens of renown, extending over several acres.

There is no record of the friendship between Joshua and Rebecca leading to courtship and marriage. Both were marrying late by Victorian custom: Joshua was over forty and Rebecca in her late thirties. They were both living in Hitchin, Joshua already at Bank House in the High Street only a few doors away from the family home in Market Square, where their long garden and Whiting's Yard ran back, parallel with what is now the Arcade. Much of that site is now covered by a spacious complex of retirement flats, suitably called Whitings Court. The handsome Meeting House where Joshua and Rebecca were married had seating (benches) for 300. There's no telling how many attended the Whiting wedding, but the Marriage Certificate (in which husband and wife make the same declaration, "promising through Divine assistance to be a loving and faithful husband/wife until it shall please the Lord by death to separate us...") carries signatures that are a roll-call of well-known Hitchin Quaker families: Ransom, Lucas, Sharples, Tuke, Allen, Shillitoe, Sewell, Latchmore, Thompson. Nearly all those names appear and come to life in the Diary and many are still to be found on plain headstones in the burial ground of Hitchin Meeting House. In today's printed list of Hitchin Friends there are only two representatives of any of the names on the Marriage Certificate.

It is impossible to keep the backgrounds of husband and wife in balance, because though there is an abundance of Whiting material, I have found very little about the Jacksons. Rebecca's father, William, came from London and was described as a 'whitesmith'. At the time of her marriage, Rebecca was already a 'recorded minister' which was the Quaker recognition of her gift for vocal ministry in a meeting for worship. It was in no way an appointment with a salary. She was to be remembered in her obituary as "cheerful and warm-hearted" and having "special care for the young". To Joshua, she was "the best of wives". Rebecca's health was a constant anxiety and there were to be no children for the Whitings but childless marriages do often have a special blessing in an extra sense of sharing, support and companionship, and this comes through to me in Joshua's diary. The code of their world was stoic and reticent, and private grief and disappointment were seldom given expression.

The Victorian Society of Friends was in many ways tribal, but within the tribes there were subtle variations of social class. The Lucas⁺ family and the Whiting family shared many generations of Quakerdom. They would have "thee'd" and "thou'd" without formality and shared in the practice of many Quaker testimonies and traditions but they would have had very different opportunities and expectations. Members of the Lucas, Tuke, Seebohm, Sharples and Exton families would have had a confident and natural expectation of an inheritance. The Whitings, the Latchmores and many other Hitchin Friends in "a middling way of life" would have been brought up to be, of necessity, self-reliant, able to earn their own livelihood and make their own way. The stories of how they did, and what happened when they didn't are full of surprise and interest. Quaker money has certainly furthered many good causes, but whether it helped the inner life of the benevolent rich is a delicate question.

Joshua and Rebecca were enviably free from anxieties about money. Not only did they seem entirely at home within the limits of their income, but they were free of the trial of responsibility (and sometimes guilt) to which wealth brought many richer Quakers. Joshua's salary at the Bank would have been well-earned and secure, but always modest. I think he and Rebecca would have felt their lives to be both comfortable and blest; his notes reflect very careful planning and spending as well as an almost child-like enjoyment of small treats, and those traits are still discernible in some Quaker families. His gift to the town and to his Meeting would have been his personality, his time, and in the constancy of his manner and his faith. In his will his legacies were to his family (including Rebecca's), his friends, his housekeeper and gardener. No causes or charities were mentioned.

A great sense of refreshment comes from the diary in its picture of the writer as so thoroughly at home in the day-to-day life of Hitchin. It is also clear that he was one of countless Quakers of his day who, though in so many ways held back by prohibitions and inhibitions, felt that in the world of nature they were free to respond

Joshua Whiting of Hitchin in the County of Hertford Baker son of

having submitting to Austin and Margaret his wife (both deceased) and

Rebecca Jackson now Daughter of William Jackson of Kingston ?

in the County of Middlesex and Rebecca his wife

having made known their intention of taking each other in Marriage to the

Monthly Meeting of Friends recommended duly held at _____ Hitchin

in the County of _____ Herts ? _____ the Proceedings of the said

Joshua Whiting _____ and _____ Rebecca Jackson _____ after due enquiry were

allowed by the said Meeting, they appearing clear of all others and having consent of

their relative Parents _____ Now these are to certify, that for the accomplishing

of their said Marriage, this _____ Eighteenth _____ day of the _____ Twelfth _____ Month,

in the Year One thousand eight hundred and _____ sixty one _____ they, the said

Joshua Whiting _____ and Rebecca Jackson _____ appeared at a public

Assembly of the aforesaid People on their Meeting House at _____ Hitchin

_____ And he the said Joshua Whiting _____ taking the said

Rebecca Jackson _____ by the hand, declared as followeth:— Friends, I take this

my friend Rebecca Jackson _____ to be my Wife, promising, through Divine

assistance, to be unto her a loving and faithful _____ Husband, until it shall please

the Lord by death to separate us. And the said _____ Rebecca Jackson

did then and there, in the said Assembly, declare as followeth:— Friends, I take

this my friend Joshua Whiting _____ to be my Husband, promising, through

Divine assistance, to be unto him a loving and faithful _____ Wife, until it shall

please the Lord by death to separate us. And the said Joshua Whiting _____ and

Rebecca Jackson _____ as a further confirmation thereof, and in testimony thereunto, did them and there to their Presents set their hands.

We being present at the above said Marriage have also subscribed our
Names as Witnesses thereunto the Day and Year above written.

| | | | | |
|---|---|---|---|---|
| Samuel Lucas | John Rawson | Elizabeth Sharples | Rebecca Jackson | Joshua Whiting |
| Joseph Marshall | Caroline Rawson | George Latimer | Daniel Mawson | Rebecca Jackson |
| Mary M. Marshall | Jane Rawson | Francis Latchmore | Thomas Latchmore | |
| Eliza Bonnet | Mary Thompson | Titus Latchmore | Maria Latchmore | |
| Catherine Tuke | Emma Priestly | | et pro Hackett | |
| Elizabeth Tuke | Mary Thompson | B.J. Rawson | Mary Whitehurst | |
| Jane Lucas | Richard Brown | Lucy Rawson | Joseph Whiting | |
| Joseph Bennett | Edward Lewell | Eliza Mawson | | |
| Anna Brown | Mary Rawson | Priscilla Rawson | Ebenezer Whiting | |
| Emily Lloyd | Marianne Lucas | Arthur Rawson | Eliza J. Jackson | |
| Lindley Tuke | John Lucas | Juliet Rawson | Lucy Wright | |
| Samuel Tuke | William Rawson | Mary Allen | John Whiting | |
| Alicia M. Tuke | Willm Brown | Samuel Allen | Anna P. Whiting | |
| Alice Richard | Aaron Hillard | Louisa Field | William Whiting | |
| Mary S Lucas | Theodore Lucas | Richard Phillips | M.A. Latham | |
| | | John M. Williams | Thomas P Latchmore | |
| | | Mary P Phillips | | |

xix

to their senses: free, in their gardens and in the countryside, to enjoy colour, form, smell, sound and touch. And in their gardens they would work as well as take pleasure, the happiest of combinations for sober non-conformists.

Joshua and Rebecca first belonged to Hitchin Meeting at a time when it was described by its most knowledgeable historian, Reginald Hine, as "sad and dying". Quaker vitality was more evident in civic philanthropy than in its Meeting for Worship, where attendance was diminishing; missionary enterprise at home and abroad, was attracting many of the most committed and vigorous younger Quakers; others, impatient of Quakerly restrictions and peculiarities were joining other denominations or becoming free-thinking radicals. In Hitchin much was done by all denominations, including the un-churched, to improve conditions for the poor of the town. Hitchin's slums were notorious and local misgovernment over many years had resulted in a dangerously sub-standard water supply and as a direct result, a shameful story of ill-health. Many societies and clubs were formed to help in the education and independence of the poor, and, for much of the nineteenth century, Hitchin Quakers were at the forefront of such enterprises, having a zeal for betterment, confidence in their role as social pioneers, and from the banking families in particular, a great deal of money to back their philanthropy.

I have the impression that none of the meetings that Joshua and Rebecca served so loyally and lovingly was flourishing or growing. The picture of small, struggling meetings recurs all over the country at this time, particularly in rural districts, and the situation may have owed much to the period of near-schism earlier in the century. In the 1830s the Society of Friends had been shaken, almost riven, by what came to be known as the Beaconite controversy. The lead was taken by an impressive, powerful group of Friends strongly attracted by the fervency of the evangelical movement that was energising the religious life of the country, and their intention was to bring the Society of Friends into line with its theology. The evangelical movement insisted on the literal truth of the Bible, emphasising mankind's original sin, with the certainty that the hope of redemption and forgiveness could only come through Christ's atoning death. The power and vitality of the evangelical movement (and, perhaps, its certainties) attracted many Friends away from Quakerism to join, in the main, the Anglican Church, Unitarians or Plymouth Brethren.

Darwin's *On the Origin of the Species* (1859) struck an instant (and still resonating) blow on the age-long reliance on the literal truth of the Bible, that told of the world's creation in six days and the fall of humankind from the eating of the forbidden fruit. Scholars, theologians, scientists, economists and philosophers across the western world were questioning and researching ever more widely and deeply. In the same year John Stephenson Rowntree published *Quakerism Past and Present*, calling for much-needed reforms within the Society, but it was not until 1884 that, in *A Reasonable Faith*, three then anonymous Friends openly criticised the dogmatism of the evangelicals and, in Terry Hart's words, "heralded the arrival of liberal Quaker theology". Joshua's Quakerism seems blessedly untouched by theological controversy, let alone by schism.

Anyone working on 19th century social history must be hugely grateful for (and amazed by) the quality and scope of journalism in local papers, particularly, perhaps, for the value they set on the full recording of countless unremarkable but greatly valued lives. The *Herts Express* of March 20th, 1909, headed its tribute to Joshua 'A characteristic Quaker life', first describing him as "one of the few remaining links which bind us to the earlier part of the last century", proceeding to his life at the Bank, where "he won the esteem of generations of customers by his uniform courtesy and attention, and his presence was so constant that he seemed to be part of the Bank himself…" "Courting no publicity, preferring to abstain from the stress of municipal life, Mr Whiting was satisfied to live on in quiet contentment." Isaac Sharp's words at the funeral were quoted, referring to "the publicity from which he so entirely and so conspicuously shrank". Ironically, thanks to his photographer nephew, Thomas Benwell Latchmore, the figure of Joshua Whiting was to become well-known in illustrations of Hitchin's history, his stove-pipe hat, well-cut coat, trim beard proclaiming a Quakerly dignity and decorum. The simplicity of Isaac Sharp's tribute to Joshua stands out clearly from some of the fulsome words of other mourners: "wherever he went and in all he did he attracted all sorts and conditions of men to him and all sorts and conditions of men looked upon him as a friend and loved him." Working on Joshua's diary, I have felt just that, and will always look upon him as a friend and love him.

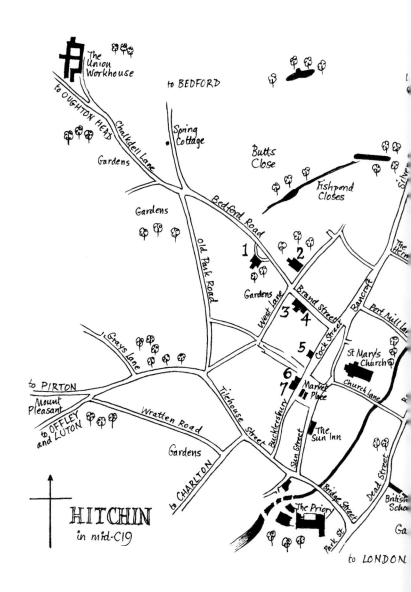

HITCHIN
in mid-C19

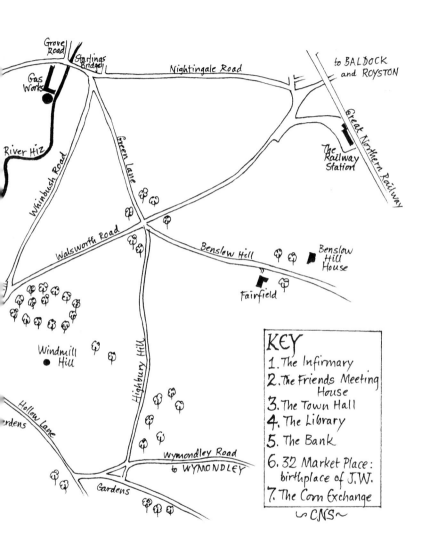

KEY
1. The Infirmary
2. The Friends Meeting House
3. The Town Hall
4. The Library
5. The Bank
6. 32 Market Place: birthplace of J.W.
7. The Corn Exchange

∽CNS∼

# 1861

**16th October[1]** – For various reasons we have decided to give up our dear old family garden at Highbury,[2] principally on account of the distance from home and the hill to ascend which is fatiguing in warm weather and takes away the little breath the Lady has – & as Thos. Latchmore† is making a new garden in his field nearly opposite the Infirmary we thought it a good opportunity to beg a price of him which he willingly gave up – in quantity about 30 poles.

Nearly half of it was overshadowed by a beautiful clump of elm trees forming in the whole a handsome head of dark foliage but as their roots would evidently make a large piece of the ground almost valueless it was decided to apply to Joseph Sharples,† the worthy owner of the ground, for liberty to cut 3 or 4 of them down and who so suitable as the Lady to ask the favour, which was kindly entertained and a promise made to inspect them in company with Philip Allen the carpenter of the estate & as the trees were decided to be too thick together, commandment was given to fell four of them, leaving three standing and one large bough of the middle one was by 'French leave' taken off also, as it was out of the line and projected over the ground.

Now came the difficulty of getting up the stumps and roots for it is supposed they had been growing about 100 years, so had got firm hold of the ground. After several days labour, the two principal ones were completely mastered by many heavy strokes. The stumps of the remaining two are left in the ground. One will form a seat and possibly the other, if required.

*   *   *   *

After many plans had been formed on paper with alterations and additions the beds and paths were finished by the beginning of November. As the summer had been a very dry one it was of no use thinking of planting till rain came, which a sudden change in the weather brought just in time. The grass near the trees has been relaid, which with the beech trees from Highbury planted near Jas. H. Tuke's† hedge are much benefited. Quite a snow storm came early in the morning of 2nd of November and it feels quite winterly.

**15th November** – Finished most of the planting so that our little plot, that a few weeks since looked so unpromising, now has a little appearance of order and a promise in the future of fruit and flowers. Brought three hives of bees from Highbury but one has apparently very few inhabitants, and is beside very light, so suppose it will not survive the winter. Daniel Pestell helped to bring the hives from Highbury – planted at the back of them a hedge of sweetbriar.

WM: *This is a good time of year for moving hives; 'very light' indicates that there is little stored honey to maintain the colony until the spring, hence the fear that it will not survive.*

**16th November** – Very severe frost for the time of year; thermometer at 18.

## 1862

**30th January** – Most of this month has been unusually mild. Aconites and snowdrops just out at Highbury – had some pleasant exercise in rolling the new garden paths. It is surprising the improvement fresh gravel paths are to a garden. We went to Tottenham for R's health a week since and Cos. William† sent a nosegay of jessamine – it is a very favourite flower of his. I gave him the plant two or three years since and one to Uncle Thomas† at the same time. William talks of raising one in a pot for the benefit of the parlour in winter time. He gave us some sweet williams and lemon thyme – planted them in the Fishponds³ garden.

The large black beetles I have seen flying about and the weather is so mild that it's little fire that is required in the Bank.⁴ The three hives of bees are alive and very active, their hum is a great addition to the cheerfulness of the garden.

**6th February** – Let our old garden at Highbury to Draper till Michaelmas – before parting with it, took up snowdrops, tulips etc. Heard the little spotted or barred woodpecker in walking round the Park. Bentley the bird stuffer told me it was 19 years since he heard it, but the shepherd says it was there last year but he did not hear its note after March.[5]

**19th February** – Observed the bees taking in farina this morning. Weather fine and open. Purchased a spud to get up the weeds that are fast making their appearance in the new garden, they were not buried deep enough to kill them. Ordered a parcel of seeds, rhubarb & potatoes, etc. from Stephen Brown of Sudbury, amounting to £1.4s.2d.

**3rd March** – A few days of very cold easterly winds, succeeded by warm spring weather.

**8th March** – Bees very busy taking in farina. The three hives appear strong – feeding one of them with honey from the "Folly"[6] taken up last Christmas.

**29th March** – For about a fortnight had a great quantity of rain so that March dust[7] has been a scarce article, but last month was unusually dry so that the usual weather has been reversed to the annoyance of the farmers who are prevented sowing barley – the land being so wet. Last week finished fencing the garden next to the Fishpond Closes – it now looks more snug and warm.

The first vegetable produce of our garden was some mustard. How pleasant to sow and reap the produce of even so small a crop! Scarcely any sunshine this month, so different to the usual bright dry weather.

**26th April** – For some days past the weather has been fine and warm so that we have no fire in the parlour. The bees are strong and busy and a hive of Bro' Joseph's[†] [Whiting] has so hung out that he put a cup on it, which is filled with them. Sister Mary[†] [Jackson] from

Chesterfield and her three girls have been spending a fortnight here. We shall not soon forget them.

Noticed this morning moths attracted by the street lights. Frank Latchmore† spoke of it as common. The spring birds mostly arrived.

WM:  *The three colonies have wintered well and are now strong. These colonies are in straw skeps, possibly with flat tops to allow supering. Bees hanging out is a sign that they are likely to swarm before long; the colony has built up in numbers and there are too many workers to complete the necessary tasks. The traditional skeppist would wait for the swarm to emerge, hive it, allow it to build up, and hope for a surplus of honey. Brother Joseph's cup is most probably a super (= cap) placed on top of an improved skep. Joseph may well have used a crockery cup, but there is no evidence of this as a habit of other beekeepers of the day.*

*A 'super' is any kind of container (straw, glass, wood) which is placed above (super) the brood-chamber, so that the bees can fill the super with surplus honey above the heads of the bees living in the brood-chamber. In modern bee-keeping a metal queen-excluder is placed between brood-chamber and super so the queen is confined to the brood-chamber. The skep is made flat-topped with a hole in the centre so that a second, smaller skep can be added above it.*

*This allows a degree of separation of brood and stored honey; producing a cleaner food product, and allowing a crop to be taken without disrupting the brood or killing the bees by fumigating with sulphur. Instead of a straw super, by this time glass bell-jars were being used; Joseph may well have used a crockery cup. By giving the surplus workers more space the colony may be deterred from swarming and encouraged to build comb for honey storage.*

*Bee-keepers at this time could be broadly divided into 'gentlemen' and 'cottagers'. The former were able to commission wooden hives and accessories from the village or estate carpenter, and may have been more interested in the scientific and educational aspects of bee-keeping; the latter may have depended on their bees providing food or a surplus to sell for cash, the extent to which they could exploit improvements in hive design would have depended on their skill and resources.*

**19th May** – The past fortnight in this month spent with Rebecca at Hastings. Most of the time while I was about the weather was dull here and a great deal of rain, but the last week has been quite summery, so that the garden is looking very promising for fruit, (considering it is a <u>new</u> garden) vegetables and flowers.[8]

We have had lettuces for some time past and I have seen none so fine. The peas look very promising – Stratton's Dwarf and the next early in flower only two rows planted together (the late ones in separate rows) and each pea planted by itself. I see in T. Latchmore's garden, Jesse Knight has sown them thick together and several rows also, that they are drawn up and only in flower at the top of the sticks. The onions are but very thin. Purchased of both the Fells† bedding plants, verbenas etc. but find Fells at Highbury has much the strongest.

As the fencing of the garden has cost £12.14s.1d⁹ decided not to build the summer house this year, so got Jesse to make an arbour and planted round it carnations, nasturtiums, etc. But think I must get a piece of matting to keep the sun and rain off.

The beans (Windsor) next year might be planted in the row with potatoes. The grass plot is much improved with the cuttings it has had and rolling. Jno. Farmer† gave me some clover seed, etc. to sow on it but am afraid not much has grown. The bees have not swarmed, two hives look well. There have been swarms on 1st May.

**9th June** – Two hives have swarmed but no casts. The weather for some time past has been cool and showery. The garden looks promising. Peas almost ready and a good succession coming on, a few gathered for Lucy Wright of Chesterfield when playing with us last week – not a cup full, when boiled they were so small.

The blackbirds etc. find out the strawberries. Our neighbours are much troubled with caterpillars in gooseberries, but few have appeared with us. The annuals are a disappointment – some are not worth looking at – some of our wild flowers are splendid compared to them.

**14th June** – Weather still very showery. T. Latchmore's hay cut a week and not yet got into cocks. Dug some new potatoes this evening, 30 to the root – seed from Sudbury. A good prospect for apples. Hive casts today – gave them to TL to help to stock a double honey hive with.

WM: *JW is aware that other bee-keepers' colonies have swarmed. Swarming is the natural process whereby the colony is able to reproduce. Although modern research allows us to understand swarming, it is still not possible for a bee-keeper to predict exactly what each colony will do. Samuel Bagster, publishing* The Management of Bees *in 1834, identified the causes of swarming as excessive heat due to overcrowding, and lack of space. (Detail of cover overleaf.) The*

*building of new queen cells and wax production by workers were known as indications of swarming. JW refers to 'swarms' and 'casts'. The swarms are prime swarms, normally issuing when the first new queen cells are on the point of being sealed; they therefore include the existing or old queen, and include a large portion of the worker-bee population. A prime swarm is therefore able to build quickly and will usually yield a honey crop in the same season. Casts are subsequent swarms, or after-swarms, and include one of the young, unmated queens, and fewer bees. Casts are unlikely to build up to produce a honey surplus in the same season, and may perish if the weather is poor and the queen is not mated quickly.*

*The 9th June comment about 'no casts' again shows awareness of the importance of the prime swarm for successful honey production. The 14th June report "hive casts today" is consistent with the prime swarms reported about a week earlier. Two, perhaps more, casts may have emerged and hung out. There was probably time to decide what to do with them. At least two casts were used to stock Thomas Latchmore's double hive. This double hive was probably two boxes put together so that the two casts were united; one of the queens would have been killed, creating a stronger colony. True double hives in which two separate colonies are operated together were little known at this time.*

**21st June** – The longest day, but how cold and dull. Glad to have a fire in the Bank – but little sun and frequent showers for some time past so that the bees have a very poor prospect for honey – gathered a few May Duke cherries.

**25th June** – Monthly meeting.10 Edward White and Joseph Morris† of Ampthill11 had tea with us, the former had 'bee fever' as dear father would say – he gives a poor report of the honey season at Ampthill and prognosticates a dull, cool, showery summer. An appearance of fine weather this evening – and so it proved.

**12th July** – Weather still very cloudy, often cool and slight showers. Caterpillars very numerous, only by perseveringly looking over the gooseberry trees are they kept down.

**16th July** – Left home for Ampthill while Sefton Hagen and wife went for their holiday – quite a change in the weather for the better, but often windy which has been the case all summer.

Monthly meeting here at Ampthill – the other day Geo. Latchmore came over to declare his "intentions". John,† Alfred and Jane Ransom and sister Maria to dine with us. Joseph and Elizabeth Sharples called after dinner. Walked with Edward White to Steppingly to see old Scott and his bees – amused at the two deaf men talking together. It is a bad season for him as he partly depends upon the produce of his hives for his living. In the winter he makes a bower in a wood and shoots wood pigeons. Rebecca went the first time with me to see him and rode a donkey. Cos. William spent a few days at Ampthill with us. While he was there got up a Pic Nic12 to Houghton Ruins but showery weather had commenced so we thought it prudent to engage the shepherd's cottage for taking tea in and well we did for it was cool and before we left it came on to rain. Cos. William very kindly would go and fetch the bus13 for the ladies – Jane Walker thoroughly enjoyed it and thanked us for the treat almost before it had begun. She rode up in a fly with Maria Morris, Rebecca, & Cos. William.

The autumn has been fine and crops of corn good. Apples and pears abundant. Our garden has been very gay all the summer. The *Phlox Drummondii* especially admired. Blue lobelia effective. Took up one old hive with some good honey in it and formed another to the two weakest left for next season. Shaw and his son have put up a substantial summer house made all of oak including the floor. King of Gosmore thatched it with straw so that it is a very snug affair, but roomy also.

The summer house had not been finished long before rats and mice took possession of it but ferrets, poison and traps have about got rid of them. Sharp frosts in November, December mild – much rain and wind.

WM:   *The comment on bee fever "as dear father would say" suggests that bee-keeping was known to the family long before JW started this diary.*
*Old Scott is an interesting character; I suspect JW was interested in finding out whether this old cottager had secured a better honey crop than other bee-keepers in the area.*
*"Took up one old hive" means that he took the surplus honey from this hive, presumably by fumigating. The weaker colonies, weakened by uncontrolled swarming with casts, were united in the hope that they could survive the winter and give a yield the following year.*

**A Quaker pic nic at Ravensborough – Samuel Lucas**

# 1863

**3rd January** – The New Year opens mild and fine. Our nosegay consists of wallflowers, Xmas rose, violets, jessamine and anemones. R. Brand leaves the Bank this day – what changes I have seen in it!

**26th January** – Went to William Fells' and chose an American Crab Tree and a Dutch Mignonne apple. The former Rebecca planted on the middle of the grass path using the spade most manfully in getting to the roots manure and earth while I held the tree and now it is staked we think it is an improvement to the garden. The apple is grafted on a long stem so long that the lady complains she shall not be able to reach the fruit – hope it may be a protection to the boys stealing them.

**29th January** – Just had supper of a plentiful supply of spinach grown in our own garden in the open border under the fence, gathered by the good lady. We have had the mildest January within the memory of man, but a good deal of rain and very strong winds most of the month. Aconites, snowdrops, violets and the early crocus out.

**12th February** – Weather very fine and but little frost. Planting potatoes by the fence and protecting rhubarb that is just coming up with matting. Raised the crab tree upon a mound the other day. It is an improvement to the grass path.

Rebecca, without consulting me, went to Fells' and bought a Ribston apple and dwarf cherry tree (May Duke), chose the spot, and planted them herself – and getting the manure also. The place for planting them was well chosen so they are an improvement to the garden.

**28th February** – Very fine weather, but little frost. Garden gay with crocuses, etc. A blue squill out – very beautiful.

The hives of bees alive and strong – feeding one. Must give them water also.

WM: *It is a pity that JW does not tell us how he feeds the bees. Nowadays this would either be with syrup made of pure refined sugar and water, or honey stored from the previous season. Bagster claims "a little stale honey, which may be purchased at a very low rate" as the best food; others suggest more exotic recipes, including beer and brown sugar. Water is needed by bees to break down granulated stores; bee-keepers should ensure that their bees have access to water, especially in Spring.*

**18th March** – Real March weather, more frost this month than in January. A nosegay of almond blossom on the table. Rebecca gathered first rhubarb today.

**20th March** – Finished sowing the asparagus bed with seed. Think in the end it will answer better than asparagus plants. This last summer was almost a failure.

Several plants of verbena have stood the winter with very little protection and the autumn planted annuals are generally alive. Nemophila just coming into flower.

**28th March** – Blackthorn just in flower. Wind strong but rather westerly. Virginia stock very gay, double furze out, and violets, anemones also.

**3rd April** – Good Friday, almost a summer day, went to Barton, tea at Hexton.

**16th April** – So far a most delightful April month, most days sunny and warm with but little frost at night with less rain than usual. Bees of course very busy, early strawberries just coming into blossom. A few shoots of the vine show the embryo blossom also. Rain wanted for the asparagus seed – put toppings in the three hives.

**20th April** – Started for Falmouth to visit A. Willmore.† Returned home 9th May, the whole time we were out no rain fell so found the garden very parched and many things dead for want of water and from a sharp frost that destroyed the potatoes, etc.

**11th May** – Rain has come at last, hope in time to save the strawberry crop and give the peas a splash.

**31st May** – Very dry weather again for two weeks or more, so that everything is suffering for want of rain. <u>Our</u> garden is gay with annuals planted last autumn, nemophila, clarkia, etc and a few self sown sweet peas are in flower.

No swarms yet. The toppings are full of bees; one hive is getting heavy. A violent storm for about 10 minutes of hail and rain a fortnight since.

WM:    *"Put toppings in the three hives" I presume indicates that glasses were added to give space to inhibit swarming. Perhaps the diary allowed JW to anticipate what should happen; he knew the season was well-advanced: "Good Friday, almost a summer day".*

**3rd June** – Two swarms today. T. Latchmore kindly hived them as I could not leave the Bank, it being Monthly Meeting, and D. Lloyd gone to London. Removed the old stocks and put the swarms in their places hoping it will prevent casting. Some combs in the toppings. Very dry weather still, every morning engaged in watering to keep things alive.

WM:    *Having secured two swarms from his hives (albeit with the help of TL) JW had scope to manipulate the colonies. The old stocks, i.e. those from which the swarms had issued, were moved away, perhaps 10 yards. Those bees that had been flying would return to the original site where the swarm was now placed, augmenting the swarm. Young, house or nurse bees would remain with the old stock to raise a new queen, and, weakened by the loss of the foraging bees, would be inhibited from producing further swarms, i.e. casts.*

**25th June** – Showers have fallen for the last three weeks. Vines in flower. Sister Ellen with us – proved to me how sweet they smell. TL busy with his hay – the very dry spring has made it late – promised a good honey season.

**3rd July** – Fine warm weather – two or three ekes seem likely to be filled – limes coming into flower.

WM: *Joshua uses the word "eke" interchangeably with "super". He uses both words to indicate a container placed on top of the hive in which the bees can build extra combs in which to store their (surplus) honey. The bee-keeper harvests the honey in the ekes/supers. Ekes can also be added beneath the hive to increase space. Bagster describes storeyfying systems: either supering by adding space above the brood or nadiring by giving space below.*

**9th July** – Took two ekes of honey to Neighbour and Son weighing 14 lbs at 1s 6d per lb. Very warm and dry, the garden parched for want of rain. Early strawberries dying off. Jno. [Whiting]† and Anna [Rebecca]† and all the children at Joseph's.

WM: *George Neighbour (1784-1865) became a Quaker as a young man, joining Westminster Meeting and becoming a very active member. From starting in business as a tea-trader and oil and paint merchant he developed an outstanding business with his sons, George and Alfred, as suppliers of bee-keeping appliances. The firm exhibited at the Great Exhibition of 1851 and had outlets in Regent Street and High Holborn. Alfred was an apicuturalist with an international reputation. It is very possible that the bee-keepers of the Whiting and Latchmore families would have come to know the Neighbours personally.*

**15th July** – St Swithin's. No rain yet and but very few clouds, nothing but sun all day for about three weeks. Grapes getting a good size, thinning the bunches. Rebecca gave a hive that had swarmed to Chas. Silcocks our town missionary.

**21st July** – Rain at last but not much. TL took another eke to Neighbours for me 7½ [lbs] at 1s 4d with a box of his own about 40 lbs.

WM: *The ekes sold to Neighbour weighed 7 to 7½ lbs. This would be equivalent to a slab of honeycomb about one foot square occupying a volume of maybe 200 cubic inches, suggesting the ekes were either only partly filled, were rather small, or were glass caps. Neighbour reported 1863 as a very good season, consistent with the price falling from 1s 6d to 1s 4d in less than two weeks.*

**31st July** – Watering many things in the garden. Wheat crops never better, no disease among potatoes or gooseberry caterpillars worth mentioning. Many bedding plants have grown but little.

Raspberries fine as usual with most they are small, a few apples on. Unusually little thunder this summer.

**8 August** – To Ampthill to liberate[14] S. Hagen, the first fortnight very warm – a Pic Nic to the Houghton Gardens. Mrs Cricks – fine apricot trees and morello cherries. A good honey year for old Scott – called when he had 13 glasses large and small on his table. Letters from Thomas[†] [Whiting] about his Ligurian bees – sent some by post. Disappointed in the size of them.

WM:   *Neighbour and Sons, working with the Exeter bee-keeper T. W. Woodbury, was the first importer of Ligurian Queens in 1859. The native British bee,* Apis mellifera mellifera, *the 'British Black', is adapted to our wet climate, being able to fly at low temperatures and withstand adverse conditions by maintaining a low level of activity. The Ligurian, or Italian bee,* Apis mellifera ligustica, *is more prolific, capable of building a large colony and therefore potentially capable of building a large surplus of honey, but cannot survive so well in poor conditions. I do not think it is coincidental that 1859 was also the year that Charles Darwin published his work on evolution by natural selection. There was considerable interest in how a species should be defined; was each species immutable, having been the subject of special creation, or could new species be created by hybridisation? By the late 1860s there were good records of* mellifera/ligustica *hybrids giving huge yields. Even though Mendel had carried out his famous experiments by this time, the basis of genetics was not recognised for many years. It is likely that the hybrid vigour of these first crosses was quickly noticed; the less favourable characteristics of 'mongrels' had yet to be appreciated.*

*Here, and again in the entry for 13th May 1864, Thomas Whiting appears to be the mentor and Joshua the enthusiastic pupil. That Thomas should acquire Ligurian bees so soon after their introduction tends to confirm a link with Neighbours, and he seems more in touch with new ideas, telling Joshua about driving and feeding bees.*

*Driving bees is described at length by Dr. Edward Bevan in* The Honeybee, its Natural History, Physiology and Management, *published in 1838; he notes that it is not so widely used as it should be.*

*"Over the hole in the hive" tends to confirm that JW was using ordinary straw skeps.*

*JW tells us that he received £1.18s for honey during 1863. He sold 21½lbs to Neighbour's for which he was paid £1.11s. It appears he sold the honey to Lucy and Elizabeth for just 6d per pound.*

**22nd August** – Bro' Thomas came to Ampthill this day. At Meeting morning and evening address read. Query how much better to have them read early in the Meeting rather than at the end? Walked to the Houghton ruins with the Miss Whites in the evening – Thomas lodged at their house.

On Saturday, T & I went to call on old Scott – with him for an hour or more. Brought out some of his beautiful glasses of honey – proposed for Benwell to photograph the cottage. Scott seemed pleased with it. Heard from T that driving bees was easily done; recommends feeding from an inverted bottle placed on a piece of zinc over the hole in the hive – very dry weather all the time at Ampthill – a change to showers about 24th August.

**10th September** – Still showery so that the farmers find it difficult to get the late barley in. The wheat crop splendid. For a fort-night past we have expected every day to find the swifts take their departure but very remarkable they are still here. This morning they were screaming almost like summer time. I have watched them many years but never knew them to stay until September before.

Took up a swarm and cast, the former very heavy full of beauti-ful white comb and honey – sold to Lucy Ransom 4 lb, to Elizabeth Lucas 10 lb. Received for honey this year £1.18s.

**Threshing barley**

The majority of the swifts left us on the 10th and remainder excepting <u>one pair</u> on the 16th or 17th. I had supposed all had gone and was not a little surprised two or three days after to see a single one and a couple perhaps twice – notwithstanding the wet and cold and a severe hailstorm, they continued with us. Nothing but having young ones I concluded could keep them and so it proved I believe, for on the 7th of October I had the pleasure of seeing three together on going to the garden before breakfast. Fras. Lucas[†] was not a little surprised at seeing from the Bank windows two of them, they left a day or two afterwards.

Bought of James Raves ground on the Bedford Road 100 feet frontage by nearly 390 feet in depth for £250.

**13th November** – Not much rain has fallen this autumn. On the tea table for some market days past we have had some good nosegays so that Fras. Lucas remarked last time it looked like summer.

**21st November** – Decided last evening to plant an orchard[15] on the Bedford Road ground, so Jim Brown commenced before break-fast with getting from Bro Joseph's a load of good manure unwashed by rains. Clark supplied nine apple trees and W. Fells three and as I could not superintend the planting of them, Rebecca started soon after dinner (notwithstanding the rain and wind also giving up her usual rest at that time) to decide where the different kinds were to be planted. Right well she did her task holding them while Brown filled in manure and earth giving him also sundry pieces of good advice at the same time. About an hour after they were planted came a storm of heavy rain which will settle them. Pears and plums must be planted next week.

**28th November** – Planted pears and plums as per list. As the soil is chalky I suppose the latter will thrive the best.

**9th December** – A thought struck me the other day, it would be a good plan to divide the gardens by beech hedges – as fencing of all kinds is so expensive. So we have commenced in earnest planting about six inches apart with sweet briar hedges dividing the orchard from the garden.

**16th December** – Finished planting the hedges of beech, 1,450 required for them. The weather continues remarkably open and mild. Rebecca brought a nice nosegay of chrysanthemums from the garden today. Xmas roses out in flower for some time.

Weather fine to the end of the year which all through has been remarkable for dryness. Many wells dry that have scarcely been known before. A remarkably large yield of wheat particularly on the middling soils.

# 1864

**January** – Sold Mr Seymour, carpenter, the middle piece of Bedford Road ground 33 feet wide and 240 feet deep for £110. Very severe frost for about a week – had a few hours skating on the Park River[16] – still short of rain.

**8th February** – Mild weather, heard the call of the partridge this evening in the orchard. Jim Brown employed in making the line of beauty[17] walk to the top of it.

**23rd February** – Charlton sold this day to F. D. Radcliffe† for £2,570 – attended the sale at the Sun Inn.

**26th February** – Sale of household goods farming stocks etc, the dinner wagon that stood in the entrance hall made £4. Mary Burr told me Edward only gave 4s 6d for it about 30 years since. Went to see the sale in the afternoon – a great concourse of people – the whole place looked miserable. The last lots sold were the bees; nine hives.

WM:   *It seems that the live bees are always the last item in a sale.*

**28th February** – Some very cold easterly winds of late. Gardens unusually bare of flowers. Still short of rain – only sprinkling showers – many wells dry in the town.

**29th February** – Leap Year – Continual rain at last most of the day, so it is still 'February fill dyke'. Seymour's house on the Bedford Road is rising rapidly into sight, the arrangement of it looks very convenient so far – shall we ever <u>progress or inhabit it</u>?

**13th March** – Much rain and snow for some days at the beginning of the month so that the spring is quite backward – weighed the four hives of bees and found all but one heavy for the time of the year. Noticed a blue squill out today.

**15th March** – Planted at orchard and old garden, Stratton's early potatoes.

**25th March** – Good Friday – almost a summer's day, as last year. Rebecca & I with the help of R. Braund's pony and chaise went first to Offley to see Lady Salusbury's orchard house, in length 130 feet, the <u>materials only</u> cost £32. One peach tree last year had 130 peaches on. The difficulty is to keep the trees from over bearing. Then to the Dyke over Lilly Hoo and on to the Red Lion at Hexton – walked by the brook and Ravensbro' Castle to the top of Barton Hills and back again to the Inn to tea. The charge for parlour and bedroom for one week is only seven shillings – when shall we go? Spring backward – no blackthorn out.

**22nd April** – Blackthorn generally out – the spring backward – all the trees in the orchard alive. Put in asparagus seed again a few days since. Our visit to Hexton was accomplished last week much to our enjoyment and benefit. We started on Wednesday 13th, with beautiful weather. I returning to business 7th day morning, walked back to breakfast on 1st day and home again on Monday. Rebecca staying till the following 5th. We stayed at Mrs Moister's cottage at the back of the Red Lion, a very great comfort in every respect to what we are accustomed to. We had our meals with the door wide open, the aspect being about south west and a bright sun all the time with birds singing, a blackbird in particular was very melodious. We had many bracing walks to the Barton Hills etc. and I hope it will not be the last visit to the kind.

**6th May** – Last month was a very dry one so that April showers seemed to be things of the past, but May set in with some refreshing rains and with absence of frost and east winds the garden is beautiful. The Highbury tulips have come out in their old colours, the white ones are much admired. Pear blossom was most profuse and apple blossom, just now in perfection, is equally so. Noticed in one hive today the drones for the first time this season. Most of the annuals destroyed by last winter's severe frosts, but many plants of clarkia escaped and will soon be in flower, so they are very hardy.

**7th May** – Saw the first swifts this morning – one pair.

**8th May** – Several swifts were flying high and screaming. Sharples begun to put a fence round the plantation on Windmill Hill – what a change it will make!

**13th May** – Walked to Ley Green to enquire if it was true there had been a swarm of bees the beginning of May. Found it was correct. Squires at the Plough Beer Shop was the owner of them, he had never known a swarm so early – Jn. Buck of the Fox, King's Walden, was my informant. I have noticed much more than usual the bees busy in the buttercups, both farina and honey. The former does not appear to be put much into their baskets but their bodies are covered with it. Brother Thomas sent me Langstroth's *Treatise on the Hive & Honey Bee.*

WM:   *1864 was another heavy-yielding year.* A Practical Treatise on the Hive and Honey-bee *was first published by Lorenzo Langstroth in 1853. Even today, Langstroth is frequently credited with "inventing (or discovering) the bee space" and giving us modern bee-keeping with moveable frame hives. He certainly played a great part in popularising the ideas, and his book had a wide readership, his contribution being readily acknowledged by Alfred Neighbour, George Neighbour's son.*

**24th May** – Last week very hot weather for some days over all parts of England, succeeded by a severe thunder storm and north wind. So cold was it that we had a fire in the Bank today. No swarms yet, the hives are getting heavy and toppings worked in.

**1st June** – Very cold to the end of May and but little rain last month. Bees have not yet swarmed.

**7th June** – The first swarm today left an eke half filled with comb.

**8th June** – Another swarm leaving an eke partly filled also – warm weather again from the beginning of June but no rain. Strawberries etc. much in need of rain. The second swarm put into the box.

A good deal of dull dry weather from middle to end of June so that the bees have only swarmed two hives out of the four and no casts. TL has had no casts from his three swarms – a very unusual circumstance.

WM: *JW notes that swarms have departed even though the ekes (= supers) are only part full; clearly, lack of space does not provide a full explanation of the swarming urge. He also seems puzzled that casts have not followed the swarms this year.*

So work the Honey Bees,
Creatures, that by a rule in Nature, teach
The art of order to a peopled kingdom.—*Shakspeare.*

**Frontispiece from Langstroth's *Treatise***

**2nd July** – Sister Mary from Chesterfield and three children with us. A better crop of strawberries than most of our neighbours and raspberries very fine and plentiful. Peas, excepting Stratton's Early, much injured by the sparrows when coming up. The garden has been very gay with roses, but those by the hedge still blighted.

**16th July** – Took large eke from hive that had not swarmed weighing 15 lbs of honey and Scott's eke 11 lbs also one eke with 4 lbs and small one 6 lbs – total 36 lbs.

**21st July** – With Daniel Pestell's help, took two hives sulphured one swarm, 20 lbs and one old Scott's for Sister Anna weighing 22 lbs, also sent her Scott's eke 11 lb at 1s 3d full and hive at 4 [*lb*] to £1.1s.1d plus large eke 15 [*lbs*] at 1s 3d; 18s.9d sold to Neighbours – [*total*] £1.19s10d.

WM: *JW reports that he sulphurs a colony in a matter-of-fact way, although for several decades there had been a consensus among bee-keeping writers advocating more humane methods of taking honey. Samuel Bagster in 1834 gives a good description of the method: "... in the latter part of the year, having determined what hives you intend to destroy, take a linen rag and cut it into narrow pieces, about six inches long, and then, having melted beaten brimstone, dip them therein. A hole must be dug in the ground, near the hives, about twelve inches across and six inches deep: at the bottom two or three sticks crossed, over which put three or four of your smeared brimstone rags. When you have lighted them place the bees quickly over the hole, stop every opening, and the inevitable consequence will be the death of your bees, (poor fellows!) discoloured combs, and the bees' empty house."*
*This confirms that JW was using simple straw hives with natural comb at this stage.*

**21st August** – Very dry weather has continued till today when a little rain and some hail fell at last, such a drought has not been for years. Many of the beeches planted last autumn for the hedges in Bedford Garden have died. Our Fishpond Garden is almost bare of flowers. But there is a very large crop for the size of the trees, of apples, Quince Orleans, and White *Magnum Bonum* plums. Meadows are bare of grass, few turnips etc.

**19th September** – Excepting a few showers, the drought has continued till the present time but now frequent heavy rainfalls almost daily and continued to do so till the 24th. Apples are so plentiful that they are selling at 1s to 1s 6d per bushel. Potatoes generally small but on Bedford Road where manure was used they are a large size and where coal ashes had been applied they were much improved.

The swifts stayed till about 9 mo. 5th and swallows till 10 mo. 10th.

**1st October** – Rebecca gathered today 10 Scarlet Pearmain and 77 Normanton Wonder apples.

The quince bore well and were distributed to many Friends.

**November** – Gave Jno. Ransom a quantity of raspberry plants for Benslow,[18] he spoke for them in the summer when he saw them in fruit. The celery is a general failure with the very dry summer and autumn. Planted many more fruit trees and evergreens in Bedford St.

**John Ransom planting Benslow**

# 1865

**4th February** – A heavy fall of snow last month, more than for years past – glad to find the annuals are alive. The bees in wooden box died, not for want of honey, but suppose I stopped up the entrance too much – it was a pity as they were a strong stock. Sold John Day the half of orchard in Bedford St for £50 and £5 for fruit trees etc. Aconites fast coming up and snowdrops. The whole of this month frequent snow storms so that there has been more snow this winter than for many years.

WM:   *I am not sure whether these bees were in a skep inside a wooden box, or had been kept in a wooden hive. Either way, JW was unlucky. In winter, worker bees die off and are removed from the hive by workers that eventually carry them away from the hive when the weather is good enough for flight. Sometimes, the drop of dead bees is so great that the hive entrance is blocked. Very often, disease or some other failure has weakened the colony and death is only secondarily the result of the blockage; too few or too weak bees are unable to cope with the quantity of dead bees. Bees generally cope with low temperatures if their nest is dry. Perhaps JW's box was not waterproof, had poor ventilation, or poor drainage, so that dead bees were wet and blocked the entrance.*

**18th March** – The first day this month that I have seen dust, having been showery so far. And the annuals have lived through the winter and promise to make a gay spring garden, but little sunshine so far and seen no bees taking in farina, feeding two hives with honey and giving water at the top of the hive. Also for the first time using shells for want of something better.

**31st March** – March has this year been unusually cold and stormy, frequent snow so that vegetation is very backward.

**5th April** – April commenced with genial weather and today some warm rain has fallen. A blue squill out at the beginning of the month. Tho. Latchmore lost the stacks of two hives in wooden boxes, for the health of bees there is nothing like straw.

**6th April** – Saml. Allen[†] at Meeting today (Thursday) much to the surprise of all his friends – came and returned in a Bath chair drawn by Jos. Pierson, Jm. Thompson assisting.

**11th April** – Saw a sand martin at Bedford St orchard – the editor of White's *Selborne* says that they appear before the swallow. Bright sunny weather for some days. Rebecca and Maria Latchmore Jr went to Hexton yesterday. I joined them on the 4th day night previous to Good Friday. As 5th day was very fine, rode in pony cart to Sharpenhoe and dined in the fir plantation on the top of the hill – found a party of young Kidmans bird nesting. Ben joined us on Thursday evening while Daniel Davis was smoking his pipe and drinking gin and water by our wood fire. On Sunday afternoon, Robt Marsh, wife and child, Robt Kingsley (bringing cake and buns with him) and lastly J. S. Sewell[†] joined our tea party, He came over to tell Mrs Croucher of the fever the children had had – it was a great blank to him to find Mrs C. dare not have them. I called at Thos. Smeetleys[?] at Wellbury on my returning on Tuesday before breakfast they would have gone there but youngest child now has fever which ended in her death in a few days.

Showery weather and very warm. Garden gay and bees very busy.

**17th April** – Plum blossom just coming out very full.

**22nd April** – Purchased three ekes of Tarrier of Snailsworth larger than I have had them before, <u>if</u> full I expect they will hold about 35 lbs of honey. TL has several times had a box of 40lb that I do not see why I should not also and I fancy the bees work somewhat in proportion to room that is given them – weight of ekes.

Poor Gudgin of Snailsworth died in the Union[19] last winter. He was much given to drink. Maria Benwell[†] tried hard to reform him, but with little effect.

**22nd April** – Splendid sunny weather – went to Spencer's garden in churchyard to see the plum blossom – a swarm of bees came last summer into a hollow of a poplar tree in his garden he hoped to get a swarm from them. Noticed potatoes stuck about his vine found it was to prevent shoots from bleeding that had been cut late.

WM: *JW seems to be buying replacements for the ekes sold with the honey; he is clearly aware that larger hives may give higher honey yields.*
*The swarm that arrived in the poplar tree had survived the winter; many modern bee-keeper's believe that wild colonies can no longer survive owing to the prevalence of Varroa, a mite accidentally introduced from the Far East, and now endemic in honey bees throughout the British Isles. Secondly, the hope for a swarm indicates the traditional view that a stock is started with a swarm. In fixed-comb skep bee-keeping, this is the usual method. In modern bee-keeping, swarms are often seen as a nuisance since lost swarms represent a loss of foraging force and therefore a loss in honey production. However, a strong swarm invariably works vigorously and will often produce a good surplus in a good season. Modern bee-keepers practise artificial swarming, deliberately separating the old queen and workers from the brood when queen cells are being produced. In this way no foragers are lost and the bee-keeper has the option of re-queening the colony with the new daughter queen.*

**28th April** – This evening the wind changed to east and now very cold – A sharp frost on the 29th that injured the potatoes, etc.

**2nd May** – Much in need of rain – many wells still dry – our neighbour John Palmer† complains of his having had no water for months. Saw the first swift today. Apple blossom just coming to perfection. Virginia stock very gay but many of the tulips not in perfection – suppose for want of rain.

**5th May** – Rebecca put on the first topping on Number Three and 13th May the second on Number Two. Number One is not so strong. A good rain last week since which the beech hedge at Bedford St has come out in full leaf. There is no fear now but that it will do well.

**13th May** – Heard the first scream of the swifts tonight in the garden.

**17th May** – Saw the first drone today – heard of no swarms yet.

The elm trees are remarkably full of seed, many of them are quite brown at the top and our garden is covered with them.

WM: *Drones, the male honey bees, are reared during the swarming season. They take longer to develop than the worker and queen brood, and are mature prior to the emergence of virgin queens. Honey bees are promiscuous outbreeders, one queen mating with maybe ten drones, these moving in from a wide area. Drones are therefore an indicator of queen rearing and therefore of swarming. Joshua is clearly aware of this.*

**20th May** – Jno. and Anna staying with us on their way to Y. Meeting – a warm day, drove after tea with sister Maria & J. & A. to Wellbury and Offley.

**23rd May** – First swarm (market day, as often the case). A thunderstorm in the evening with much wanted rain. A fine warm May.

WM: *Even today, bee-keepers frequently complain that bees swarm at the most inconvenient times. When I started bee-keeping, for many years, I never encountered a swarm; my bees only swarmed when I was away with my students on our annual biology field course. This was always about the middle of July, ten days as near as possible to spring tides. Did my bees swarm earlier but I didn't notice? Was I manipulating my bees to suppress swarming which happened as soon as I was not there to cut out queen cells? Or is it that bee-keepers remember those days when there is a swarm just as they set out for a family wedding or whatever?*
*"A swarm of bees in May is worth a load of hay."*

**1st June** – Last month was a very dry one but that evening rain came on and during the night nearly one inch had fallen, but grass crops are very light, promised a good honey season – caps getting full.

WM: *Joshua clearly understands what is needed for a good honey crop: long spells of warm weather, but sufficient moisture to ensure an adequate nectar flow.*

**3rd June** – A cast today or a <u>stray</u> swarm. Jno. & A. with us returning from Y.M. gathered a few of Black Prince strawberries this evening. Surprised to find them ready. It proved to be a cast of the first swarm. The season is a very good one for bees so they may stand.

WM: *Cast swarms are produced at 9-10 day intervals after the emergence of the prime swarm. We are not told why JW deduces that this is a cast of the first swarm. If he was operating fixed-comb skeps, his opportunity for examining the colony would have been limited.*
*"A swarm of bees in June is worth a silver spoon.*
*A swarm of bees in July isn't worth a fly."*

**10th June** – Went to Ampthill on the 5th day. Eighth June noticed wheat in ear. The season is an early one. Rebecca gathered 1lb of Black Prince strawberries today. As the first toppings appear full of honey, added another to the two hives that have not swarmed. Just an eke over the swarm, they are filling it with comb. Grapes just coming into flower not so many bunches as usual. T. Latchmore cutting his grass, not much more than half a crop owing to the dry season and sharp frost of 29th April. No wasps. In the autumn the queens are said to have been killed by the frost.

**17th June** – The swarming season appears over, only Number Two swarmed and cast. The latter is quite heavy and strong with bees. A few days since put on a second topping to One and Three; Number One was open at the top of the hive all the winter for feeding and appears to have done as well as Number Three, which was closed all the same time.

WM:  *JW does not tell us what he means by "closed"; it is most unlikely that there was no roof, although bees can survive like this. The roof blew off one of my hives and the bees built a sheet of propolis almost enclosing the three by one inch hole in the crown board to keep out the rain. Modern hives are traditionally built with ventilation arrangements, but most colonies seem equally healthy with nothing.*

**21st June** – Benwell drove Rebecca to Hertford Meeting, suppose it will be the last one held there. Very hot today and yesterday but last Sunday very cold, and for some days the nights had been quite chilly, commenced thinning the grapes before tea this evening and bought a new pair of scissors at John Gatward's,† Maurice Kingsley serving me.

The lime blossoms just in flower and white jessamine.

**30th June** – A good rain at last, just in time to save many things. It will give us some good peas in the orchard.

**1st July** – Took the first topping of honey weighing 6 lbs from Number Three.

**4th July** – Took from same hive a large eke with 21 lb. Thos. Latchmore took it to Neighbours and got 1s 6d per lb also sent a second, 21 [lbs] and 10½ [lbs] at 1s 3d, received in all £3 10 shillings.

Cos William staying with us. Fred Marsh leaves for Hertford branch tomorrow.

**7th July** – A topping from Number One, 10½ lbs. A very heavy rain yesterday evening. Town flooded. J. H. Tuke's, C. E. Prince's drawing rooms injured by it and frequent showers now about. A good deal of rain for some days after – four inches in four days. Most of the trees in Bedford St. have fruit on. One codlin apple growing considerably. The damsons and plums so loaded that I have thinned them considerably. Planting strawberries to form an edging to the path up the orchard.

**15th July** – Received from Cos. William three buds of Devonshire rose – took them to Wilton but found he was from home, so from necessity, I was compelled to try my hand upon them – trust they succeed.

**17th July** – Warm weather with rain. Took a large eke from Number One, 19½ lbs, gave it to Sister Esther† [Latchmore] to divide with Anna and M. A. Tatham.

**21st July** – General Election – E. Latchmore and Esther and E. Chapman† and [wife] Mary with Thomas came to vote for [Herts MP] Cowper,[20] who was returned at the head of the poll. This has been a very warm July with heavy showers. No honey dews up to this time.

**31st July** – Proceeds of three stocks for this season: Number One – 30lbs; Number Two – swarmed and cast; Number Three – 28 lbs; and from swarm 21lbs. Total 79lbs. Received £3. 10 shillings.

The cast will also stand without feeding so this has been a good season.

WM: *Bee-keepers always seem better at recording their successes than their failures! Joshua clearly shows that those hives that do not swarm are more productive.*

**16th August** – Rebecca and I left for Ampthill. Frequent showers all the first part of the time. With one day's heavy rain that improved the wheat that was stacked but not thatched. The very large quantity of fine old wheat of one or two years old will now be in great demand as the new is generally not of first quality and far from dry.

The potato disease is much complained of, how will ours be in the orchard?

Walked to Pulloxhill, found it one mile beyond Jno. Randall's of Greenfield. It stands quite on a hill and has a fine view of Barton on the opposite side and an extensive prospect over Silsoe, Shillington, Hitchin and Stevenage, etc. If all's well this must be my last visit. There used to be a Meeting here, but closed some years since. James Brown told me he saw an old man who remembered being at a funeral. When they had stood some time by the grave in silence, a Friend said "put it in", which concluded the ceremony.

I called on Chas. Chipperfield and saw in his orchard a wonderful apple tree that measures seven feet three inches in circumference. The produce has made on an average £10 a year for many years together – producing 80 and one year 100 bushels. He has a pear tree grafted with three or four different kinds and does well. Some years since a small quantity of gold was found in a field close by Polluxhill which goes by the name of the Gold Field.

**29th August** – Walked with Edward White after an early tea at their house to Mr Platts, Bickerings Park, Ridgmont, to see the orchard where the first Yearly Meeting was held in the south of England. Jno. Crook† lived there at the time in a large old castellated house with walls a yard thick, but it was pulled down some years since and three years ago the old orchard trees were all destroyed, which I much regretted. There is still the tradition among old families in the neighbourhood for a very large Meeting being held there. In going, passed by the Midland Line now being made. Sam. [Lucas] and his wife drove by us on the road.

Saml. Seabrook asked us to go again to see his fruit etc. E. White and his wife Mary, Francis, Rebecca & I went. He had a good show of worthy plums and apples very fine, the latter pruned so as that fruit all over the tree middle as well, but the grapes were the chief object, those in the orchard house ripening well. The length is 50 yds. and only cost £20, he assisting. F. Seebohm† talks of having one like it, the great thing is in the ventilation of the house, not to have it scorching hot or much draft unless the air is warm. At the blossom time particular care is required. Snow prunes his vines close to the stem, but S. Seabrook leaves one bud and the embryo one close to

Two autotypes by Samuel Lucas:
Ploughing (top) and Hedging (bottom)

the stem but as soon as any life appears in spring, in both buds the top one is rubbed off, so that his old stems show scarcely any spurs. He recommends beside the common Hambro' Snows, Muscat Hambro' & White Sweetwater.

Went to call at Mr Scott's at Steppingly several times and Rebecca returned to Hitchin for a few days and persuaded Benwell[†] to promise to bring her back to Ampthill in his Photographic Cart but the evening before they were to start Ben found was not prepared so the good Lady had to return by rail. Much vexed with B. we both were, as I had arranged with Scott to remain at home. E. White walked over in the afternoon and found Scott quite out of temper but talking to him about his honey, etc, brought him round. About 9 o'clock pm. Ben made his appearance – we were at first inclined to be cross with him but made it up over the supper table and arranged to start early for Steppingly to see if Scott would be taken. We found him at breakfast, (but he managed to slip all into the cupboard before we entered the house) after a little talk he seemed pleased with the idea of being photographed. We soon started for Ampthill. The morning being warm and walking quick threw B. into a profuse perspiration. E. White started with him directly after breakfast and took two views of Scott at the back of his Ivy Cottage and then on to Aspley and Hogstye. They did not return till dark – had tea at Lucy Hows. Both E White and Mr Scott complain of its being a bad honey year. It's been one of the best I have ever known. E. returned home 4th September. The weather for the past week has been very fine and warm.

**11th September** – Cos. Ann Whiting staying with us. William W., Rebecca and I start for Buxton 13th September to join Thomas there – hoping to benefit his rheumatism.

The potato disease very bad with us promoted by the heavy rains during harvest.

Thomas, William, Rebecca & I spent 12 days this September at Buxton. Worked hard sightseeing most of the time. The weather all that we could wish. The whole month has been an extraordinarily fine one. The grapes are very good and a fine crop of tomatoes the first time of growing them. The garden is gay with flowers and fruit.

Old Scott of Steppingley. 1865.

Old Scott of Steppingley near Ampthill
a great beekeeper. 1865.

Also the pampas grass adds to the effect. The Scarlet Pearmain apples are a large crop and bright colour, they are just ready for gathering. Thomas tells me his three hives this summer produced more honey than mine. I cannot understand it, his being so near Sheffield.

WM: *There are several factors that may explain these different experiences. Different strains of bee, small differences in local environment, different availability of forage crops, different methods of manipulation, and incidence of disease will all have an effect? Towns may have slightly higher temperatures than the country-side, and more shelter, and, except in the most industrialised areas, a wider variety of bee forage plants. Conversely, a steel town such as Sheffield may have suffered severe air pollution that may have adversely affected the bees. Surely, some of this would have been obvious to these men.*

*A critical factor in determining the size of the honey crop is the age and vigour of the queen. If she is properly mated in her first year, she can be expected to create a strong colony the next, able to produce a good surplus. If mating is not complete (owing to inclement weather delaying mating while the queen ages) she may cease producing fertilised eggs that produce (female) workers.*

September was very unusual for continued sunshine – with only rain one day. The grapes are very fine and sweet. Many quite a golden colour. Rebecca got some tomato plants and put them against the wall in Bedford St. They are the first we have grown. They are large and abundant and many have partaken of them.

This year has been the greatest plum year ever remembered. Jno. Malden tells me a tree that generally had two or three bushels had four bushels.

October was remarkable for the great quantity of rain, upwards of seven inches falling. The average for the month being only about three inches. Grapes have been very ripe and large, the stems in them quite brown – some bunches growing in front of the upstairs parlour window became ripe also. W. French the Relieving Officer living on Hitchin Hill gave me a black grape vine which I have planted in Bedford St. near to the gate, also planted three peaches and four Moor Park apricots. The beech hedges begin to grow and the fruit trees generally flourish. The year ended with mild wet weather and a good deal of wind, which blew down part of the wall in Bedford St. Cos. William with us at Xmas time and Josh & Etty Latchmore over at TL's.

# 1866

**January** – Some quantity of heavy snow and sleet fell this month which so lodged on the telegraph wires and accompanied with high wind as to blow down a large number of the posts on our lines and many miles round London – an unheard of circumstance. The frost only lasted a few days. By the end of the month, snowdrops, violets, heath wallflowers, anemones and crocus all in full flower, even the squill is partly out.

**1st February** – All the five hives alive. Four of them have no bungs in them, the hole only covered over with a piece of comb. Purchased of Chas. Silcocks, our late town missionary, a hive of bees and two boxes with cover for £1.15s. It is stated to be proof against swarming – time will prove.

WM: *Joshua makes few entries concerning winter feeding or how he prepares his stocks for the winter. The bungs are presumably used to close the hole at the top of the straw skep. Bees can survive quite exposed to the elements, although most bee-keepers would prefer to have a good rain-proof of some sort. This was either an earthenware crock or a straw hackle. The new hive bought from Chas. Silcocks is presumably a straw skep forming a brood chamber with wooden 'supers'. These would allow more space for a growing colony, but would be unlikely to prevent swarming altogether.*

**7th February** – Still wet and very windy. Brother Thomas sent his experience of bee keeping last year to *The Cottage Gardener* from which it appears that from three stocks he had four swarms (one a virgin one weighing 8lbs 9½ oz) and took 91 lbs of pure honey from super and side boxes without a particle of bee bread. I could not have believed it possible that so close to Sheffield one half of such success could ever be obtained.

Most of February continued wet so that Lax's Pond[21] is again full of water. For about three years it has been almost and at times quite empty.

WM:    *Bee bread is brood food and clearly the importance of obtaining pure honey without any adulteration is of significance. Queen excluders, panels with holes or slots that restricted the queen to the brood area but allowed workers to pass freely, were not developed until about 1865, and not widely used until 1875.*

*Reference to 'side boxes' suggests that Thomas may have been operating bees more or less on the collateral system. Advocated by White in the 18th century and popularised by Thomas Nutt early in the 19th century, this involved restricting the queen to a central 'pavilion' in which brood was raised. This was achieved by use of slots in the walls. Lateral honey boxes were added either side, often with bell glass supers on top.*

The Cottage Gardener, Country Gentleman's Companion, and Poultry Chronicle *was published from about 1850 and was one of the principal journals disseminating ideas and developments in bee-keeping. I have two volumes for 1858 and 1860, unfortunately not that containing Brother Thomas's contribution.*

**3rd March** – The last three days we have had very severe frost and having had scarcely any all the winter, the effects I am afraid will be very bad. The annuals and verbenas that had lived through the winter I expect will have perished.

**9th March** – First day for cattle plague. Planted Little Gem dwarf peas and improved ash leaf potatoes.

**30th March** – Good Friday – and as usual a very beautiful day. Worked in the garden in the morning. Bees taking in farina and cleaning young ones. Went a ride in the afternoon to Bendish with Joseph & Rebecca also Walter and Charlie. Sarah Ann confined with a girl still born.

Sallows in blossom also blackthorn in our garden hedge.

WM:    *After a wet February and severe frost in early March, Good Friday is spring-like. The bees are bringing in pollen.*

*Sallows (L. Salix) are a low-growing species of willow, distinct from osiers.*

**3rd April** – Planting asparagus seed in the orchard trust it may succeed better than the old garden. Rebecca put in the row just to

Richardson's orchard in top bed from seed saved last autumn. The other seed was two years old.

**14th April** – Blackthorn fully out. Set peas in orchard front row, Champion of England the top of the row next to Squire's from Back St. and Green Mammoth. Geo. Latchmore said he heard the chiff chaff on Good Friday in his garden at Luton.

**16th April** – Walked to Snailsworth to order hives for Thomas. Saw a pair of swallows, the first of the season. Stormy weather just now after thunder, etc.

**19th April** – Some top shoots of the vine an inch long. Heard from Thomas that the thunder storm they had destroyed a large number of bees.

**1st May** – At Niton, Isle of Wight, saw two swifts, weather just then very cold.

**9th May** – The first drone seen today. Did not return home till the 7th so they may have appeared earlier. Quite sharp frosts – seven degrees on the 1st and 2nd. I suppose it is that that has injured the vine, as I think I never saw it look more unpromising.

**10th May** – The greatest commercial panic ever known. Overend Gurney† Co Ltd. stopped payment this day, followed by a host of others.

**11th May** – Strong high wind with heavy showers. Apple blossoms fully out. Planting bedding plants.

**23rd May** – The first swarm today. Frank hived them. The weather for a week past has been very dry with east wind and warm sun. Arthur Latchmore at home from Falmouth stung on the nose in our garden. The next day being 1st day, he had to keep indoors as it had so much swollen. Etty here and Chas. and Arthur Willmore.

WM: *Bee stings are an occupational hazard of bee-keepers, and inevitable for their family and friends. Honey-bees originate in tropical forest where they have evolved defensive strategies to protect their nest. For bee-keepers there must be a balance between 'good' defensive behaviour against wasps, ants, etc. and 'bad' defensive behaviour. Joshua does not seem to be doing any queen selection, so his strains will tend to develop these 'wild' characteristics. Even when bee-keepers acquire a selected stock, the outbreeding that is the result of essential queen rearing to maintain the colonies, will often lead to stingy bees after a few years. Most bee-keepers develop tolerance of bee stings; it is their occasional visitors that usually suffer!*

**29th May** – With exception of one shower still dry but wind westerly. Bees working well in three hives – think Re's swarm went with TL's – walked to Letchworth, bees at work on the May – light farina.

**1st June** – A heavy rain in the night – sun came out hot and so was not surprised to find two swarms. They settled near together on the favourite *Arbor Vitae* and Frank going into the garden put them into one hive. They make a very strong stock. One of the swarms came from Silcocks' box. I was rather surprised and disappointed as the two under boxes were partly filled with honey.

WM: *I suspect the* Arbor Vitae *is the favourite of the bees rather than of Joshua and Re. A bee-keeper quickly learns where swarms are likely to cluster near the apiary; conifers such as the* Arbor Vitae *are often favoured by the bees.*
*Joshua's caution about the non-swarming hive from Charles Silcock is justified. Even modern bee-keepers will place great emphasis on hive design, believing bees are less likely to swarm in one than in another. The key to controlling swarming is the way the bees are managed. We do not know the precise arrangement intended for Silcock's hive, but it is odd that Joshua speaks of underboxes; I suspect that the hive was a flat-topped straw hive for the brood with wooden boxes above as supers. Bees will tend to add honey stores above the brood. Maybe Joshua did not understand this and so used the innovation incorrectly. He was not the first bee-keeper to do this!*

**2nd June** – Two casts today joined them at night. The first really summer day. Edward and Esther came today till Monday from the Y. Meeting. Drove them through Charlton, Offley Holes and Preston. A beautiful sunny evening. The garden now is some respects in its prime, especially just after sunset. The white flowers of strawberries, peas and beans, beside rockets and other garden flowers make it very cheerful.

WM: *Both casts were led by virgin queens. After uniting them, one of the queens would have killed the other, her rival, thus producing a stronger single stock, better able to build up and more likely to yield a surplus in the first season. Uniting small swarms was advocated by some writers of the day.*

**6th June** – Thunder with heavy rain. All the six stocks that we commenced the season will have swarmed but one and some have cast, the opposite of last season, both as regards swarms and honey.

WM:  *Joshua is making sound observations here. How each colony behaves will depend in part on the age of the queen, and will change as new queens are raised following swarming.*

**9th June** – The last few days have been good for the bees. The late rain has made everything most luxuriant. It is quite a swarming season all over the town, and many the last few days flying from their homes after hiving.

WM:  *Bee-keepers are still bemused when swarms do not stay put after they are hived.*

**12th June** – Cool and windy with showers, hay making just commencing. A letter from Thomas today mentioned that he has not yet had a swarm and that they are very scarce with them, the season altogether very unfavourable near Sheffield. Gathered a nice dish of Black Prince strawberries, wonder they are not more grown.

**21st June** – Last 1st day was very cold, glad of a fire, but today has changed to heat again with a storm at night. Bees have collected little honey this month so far. Quarterly Meeting at Wellingboro' today. Rebecca gone and on to Finedon where I join her next Saturday if all's well. Had a pleasant time at Finedon; Alice Wychelly and Anne Lamb living with T. Harlock.

**28th June** – Grapes just coming into flower. Hot weather for a week past and much honey gathered. Louise Treal on a visit to us during her vacation.

**30th June** – Thunder storm today and in many parts of England followed by wet and windy and cool weather for a week.

**5th July** – Cos. William came for a visit. Curtis Latchmore and Arthur also over the way. The lime blossoms just coming into flower.

**6th July** – The gardener at Mount Pleasant[22] grafted three briars this evening – Louis XIVth close to the bees, Jno. Hopper, dark rose colour, and Madame Didot, a perfect shaped light rose, next to aspara-gus. Also on same briar on the middle stem a rose from TL's and Madame Didot grafted next to the yellow broom also.

**17th July** – Took two ekes of honey weighing together 30¾ [*lbs*] which TL carried to neighbours and got 1s 3d per lb. They both came from the only hive that had not swarmed but one of them had been put over a swarm to get quite filled which it was, to the brim.

TL is much disappointed with his ekes and glasses not having any filled but one hive that he put on is three parts filled but it has also wood comb in it.

WM:  *Thomas Latchmore as one of Hitchin's main grocers (also a confectioner and dealer in tea) would certainly have had some sort of horse-drawn conveyance for collecting and delivering, but he may well have used the railway with a cab or horse-drawn omnibus at the other end.*
*I am not sure what is meant by "wood comb". Perhaps it is the papery comb of the common wasp.*

**20th July** – Another eke weighing 10 lb from the same hive that the 30lb came from, also one from a swarm 6lb and two other ekes partly filled – 7lb – total 53 lbs. Received £2.5s. Rebecca had 18 lb in her eke that was over her swarm and cast, united sold for 1s 3d per lb.

**6th August** – A week's rain and windy weather just at the begin-ning of harvest.

**7th August** – Very high wind today which blew off a large pro-portion of our pears at the orchard and quantity of apples. Showery weather has continued.

Went to Baldock yesterday. Drove round by Great Wymondley – got to Little Wymondley by mistake and on to Graveley – by the Old North Road to Baldock. A glorious harvest day. Mary A. Steed's† flower garden very gay and all planted by her own hands.

**23rd August** – The swifts took their departure today, at least the majority of them. Rebecca fancied she saw a company of them leaving yesterday.

**24th August** – Saw a solitary pair of swifts this evening, but not afterwards.

**25th August** – Went on walk by Mr Hill's farm and green lanes between Offley and Pirton Road and was surprised to see bees upon the wild clematis getting both farina and honey from it.

WM: *This series of entries suggests that the indifferent season eventually produced a reasonable honey crop. A strong colony of bees produces perhaps 500 lbs of honey each year, but most of this is needed for their own survival. The bee-keeper can only take the surplus. His skill can maximise this yield.*
*Collecting both pollen and nectar late in the season shows that brood is still being reared. Worker bees live for about six months during winter, so breeding must continue well into the autumn if the colony is to survive.*

**3rd September** – Spent two days of my holiday in walking to Cottered and back through Willian and Weston. Strickland the Relieving Officer giving me a lift of a couple of miles on to Luffenhall. Called at a cottage where an old man had gathered some champinions, he said they were better than mushrooms. Slept at Baker's at the Bull at Cottered and then to Julien's Park and Broadfield and Red Hill Chapel, Wallington and Baldock, home. The next day started by rail to Dunstable and over the downs to Ashridge Park, over the common to Berkhampstead and slept at Rickmansworth. Sunday very wet morning, Lord Ebury's Park and on to Chalfont St Giles across fields and woods and next morning to Jordans[23] by Milton's House and cherry orchards quite timber trees. Spent two hours at Meeting House. Took the following names from the visitor's book – *Benj. Tatham & Eliz. Beck, Hitchin 21st Feb, 1831; Saml. Allen, Amersham 21st Feb, 1831, Caroline & Maria Ransom 5 July 1831, Saml. & Matilda Lucas Sept, 1838, Saml. & Phebe Allen, Hitchin, 1839.*

On returning through Chalfont St Giles, called on William Goodman, shopkeeper, quite an antiquarian and interested in Jordans. Promised him Dixon's *Life of William Penn*, which T. Latchmore got second-hand, the work being out of print. To Amersham to tea at the Griffin. Mr Drake wrote me a note recommending my staying there. A fine park and house close to the town where Mr Drake was born. Called at the almshouses to see if any of the inmates remembered Saml. Allen living at Amersham. The first old woman I saw asked me in to her very comfortable room. Widow

Adams by name and found she used to supply Saml. Allen with meat and well remembered him and Phebe A. She told me of a little circumstance that often came across her mind which was that Phebe once came to order some meat and her little boy accidentally ran against her, she thought it was rude of him and scolded him for it, but in about an hour after she returned with a book to show him she did not bear resentment. Rode by the bus that C & A Willmore recommended to Wendover and slept at the Red Lion intending to return to London the next morning by the bus, but it proved so wet that I walked to Aylesbury instead and by train to Tottenham where Rebecca was waiting for me. Next day we went with Cos. William by boat to Chelsea and walked to South Kensington Museum and the following day to the Crystal Palace by the L & Chatham Railway. One reaching home found Bro' Thomas had come a few days before to Joseph's. The weather was dull and wet most of his visit.

**24th September** – To Ampthill again. With the exception of two days it was dull and showery. Many farmers had not done harvest till the beginning of October.

Had a talk with Jos. Croxford again about the beans. He says for the last three years, including this, the eye in the pod has been downwards and for the next three it will be upwards.

Walked over to Steppingley the first time and found Scott from home. Had a chat with his next door neighbour about him and left word that I would call again. Edward White had previously complained that his cottage was not so clean as it used to be, but I found on my second visit that he had washed the floor, etc., made a wood fire and everything prepared for my visit. He soon brought out a bottle of mead four years old. It was bright and clear and very good. He would have me take it home. He screws the wooden top of his hives into the hoop that the straw is begun upon and has offered to make the lower part of a hive for me. As it was too dark to see his hives and vine I went over again before breakfast and found he had in all, indoors and out, 70 hives besides 10 or 12 at another place. Most of them he was going to take up. He had two white clover fields close by him. He described the bees as <u>shovelling in</u> the honey. I had to fill my pockets with nuts of his own gathering and he had previously bought us some peaches and walnuts, but the latter from

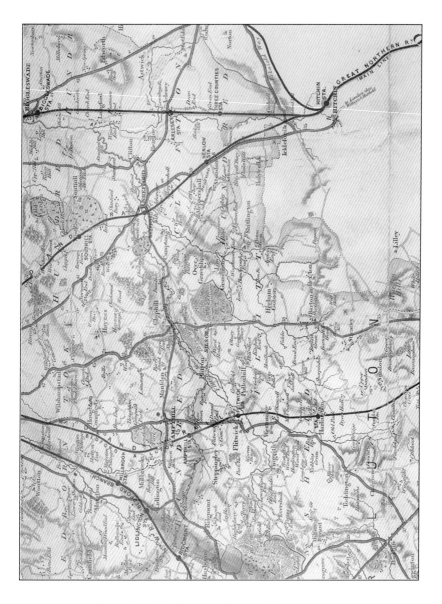

# Road and Rail: the Bedfordshire Connection

**Nineteenth century Hitchin before the growth of suburbs**

**Queen, worker and drone from Bagwell's**
*The Management of Bees*

Furze Blossom with Mason or Lapidary Bee

Wild Strawberry

Sharpenhoe and the Bedfordshire Plains

A walk at Oughton Head - Samuel Lucas

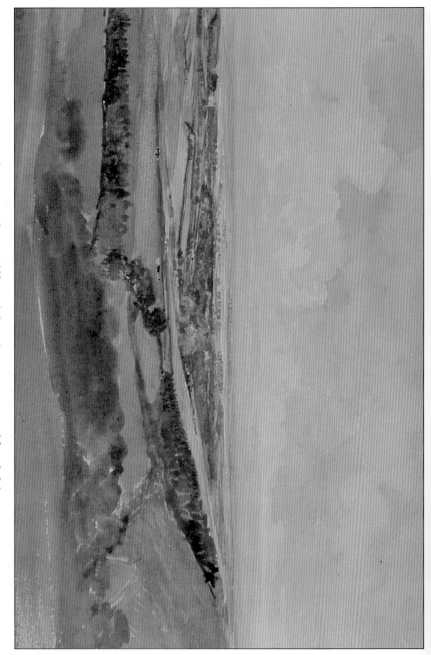

The Pegsdon Hills with view over Bedfordshire

the absence of sunshine and great moisture for weeks past are not much worth.

The last Sunday I walked to Cranfield or rather Bourne End, Thos. Grimes'. The house old and rambling and garden in character, the graves[24] almost covered with box trees, etc. Phebe Grimes lived servant she told me with the Wheelers at Saml. Allen's house and she remembered father being sent for late one winter's night in consequence of noises they heard – which proved to be the snow falling from the roof. Phebe left in consequence of a fall in going up the <u>ladder</u> to bed, there was only a rope to hold by. T. Grimes' man Jno. Foster drove me to Marston Station coming home.

Owing to the wet weather the fungi were very plentiful, some large scarlet tops and creamy white underneath. Blackberries we got a great many and bought some home. The best preserve we have ever had of the kind.

The remainder of the year was decidedly wet with but little frost. At the December Quarterly Meeting we had for our sleeping guests, Thomas Harlock of Finedon and Sarah Higham of Northampton. The former was taken seriously ill on returning home and died that day fortnight to the great regret of all who knew him. He was apprenticed to Benj. Bull Collins at Royston. Many were the anecdotes he delighted to tell of the old Friends. His manner of doing it added greatly to the interest. I am so glad we paid a little visit to Finedon this summer. The house, shop, garden and orchard with its cheerful master will long be remembered and not forgetting the thatched Meeting House and little burying ground.

WM: *Old Scott is using an 'improved' skep with a wooden crown board, allowing supering and a degree of colony manipulation. We have several illustrations of how Joshua learns what others are doing, but he does not seem sure about what <u>he</u> should do.*

# 1867

Not many days of the New Year had passed before a sharp frost set in succeeded by a thaw for a few days when the frost and snow returned with great intensity, part of the time accompanied with easterly wind which I suppose gave me a little cold on my chest, so that my good Rebecca would have me stay in doors and have a fire in our bedroom. Thanks to her kind care it gradually subsided.

**2nd February** – A beautiful little nosegay is on our table today consisting of heath, yellow and red primrose, aconite, white allysum and lovely single snowdrops. The green of it composed of variegated box, yew, <u>Ackworth</u> moss and wild ivy leaves richly marked, all gathered by the Lady.

**16th February** – The blue squill out today, very mild for the time of the year all the hives alive and feeding most of them. Farina taken in yesterday.

**1st March** – Heard the woodpecker the other day when in the garden. It is to me a new note in the Fishpond Closes. Found some bees on the path under the plum tree that grows close by the hives headless and stomachless, they must have been the remains of a tomtit's feast. Sent them to Sheffield. The month opens with easterly wind and frost at nights which is fortunate as things were getting very forward. Almond blossom just ready to burst.

**7th March** – Joseph S. Sewell, Lewis & Sarah Street † started this day from our station for Madagascar. Josh. Sharples and William Ransom and wife going with them to see them on board the 'Roman' at Southampton. Also Lucy Neild, and Lucy† [Sewell to become Johnson] & Hannah Sewell went with their father. I went down to see them on station. Just before they started it came on a very heavy hail storm. J. Sewell's last sermon on Sunday afternoon was from 2nd Corinthians, Chapter 13 verse 11. The next day nearly 50 Friends met at Jno. Ransom's to tea, a farewell Meeting to the Madagascar party. Alf. Ransom read the 12th Chapter of Romans and then followed beside address from JS and L. Street, prayers from Alfd. & William Ransom, Lucy Nield, Margaret May, Caroline Read and Fred. Marsh. It was <u>suggested</u> that the Bible should be read in <u>all</u> our Meetings for worship.[25] What will be the result and fruits of it if carried out?

**15th March** – Edward & Arthur L. came yesterday. Edward to assist Thomas at stocktaking, the result was unexpected to us. Rebecca went with Esther to London to consult Dr Phillips, 40 Harley St. He gave Sister more encouragement than we expected. Gout is the great source of her ailments – recommended her to lead an active life.

**18th March** – The weather most of this month has been very wintry. Severe frost two nights and snow storms frequent. The large tomtit feasts upon many of our bees, the remains of them scattered on the ground under the damson tree close by the hives.

**22nd March** – Break up of the frost at last. The wallflowers are mostly destroyed by the severe weather. Broccoli and greens have also shared the same fate.

**Rabbit drawing by Samuel Lucas**

**27th March** – A note came from Jane Ransom this morning inviting us at her father's request to take tea with them once more, which we did this evening. After the long cold weather that has just left us and the thorough change in temperature and bright sun made Benslow very beautiful, but there was a melancholy feeling about the place as the master is not expected to live many weeks. Rickman Shillitoe† and Dr Phillips saw him yesterday and pronounced the disease in his throat to be again increasing and they do not recommend a third operation. We found him very chatty and active and to see him it was impossible to picture the sudden change that <u>may</u> occur very shortly.

**11th April** – To Quarterly Meeting at Luton. Sister Mary from Chesterfield and Edith & Emily with us. T. Latchmore drove Mary & Rebecca, I walking on to Lilley and a <u>very windy</u> journey we had of it. Dined at Robt. Marsh's and tea at George Latchmore's.

**16th April** – The first swallows seen by me today, weather very windy still and wet. Blackthorn fully out a few days since.

**19th April** – Good Friday – A beautiful day walked with sister Ellen & Edith to Wain Wood26, took our dinners with us and Gyp also. Before entering the wood met some boys with hands full of primroses. Edith was afraid they had gathered them <u>all</u>, but was soon greatly surprised to see parts of the wood almost covered with them. Got home at 4 o'clock, a nice tea with stewed rhubarb from our garden and eggs from Chesterfield ready for us. Continued wet till the end of April. Lax's Pond full of water – a very unusual circumstance of late years.

**3rd May** – Quite a summer's day. Bees getting strong; seen no drones or swifts yet. Tulips and cherry blossom in perfection, not much apple; pear and plum has been very abundant; there has been but little frost so expect they will be plentiful. Papering the dining room – 2d per yard.

**4th May** – Sunday – In the Burying ground saw the first swifts this season. Alfred Ransom† gave the boys at the School today an eloquent address on the beauties of nature in spring. His quotations were rather liberal from the poets. Another warm day.

**5th May** – Warmer than any day yet this spring. Called on old Spencer in the Churchyard, found him in his garden dusting some seedlings with <u>sawdust</u> to drive away the slugs – it was recommended to him by Wm. Impey of Dead St. He has had a swarm of bees in a poplar tree for two or three years. This spring Frank Latchmore has contrived to make them go through a hive full of empty comb hoping to entice them in. Drones seen by him yesterday. Sent asparagus to Aunt Ann Shillitoe† she being very ill.

Very warm weather lasted for a week and then came a great storm of thunder and lightning, rain and hail which made it unsettled for some time. Ponds and ditches are full of water.

**17th May** – heard from Jno. Edwin Eddison of the death of our old friend Mary Ann Tatham, she died at Southport and was bought to Leeds to be buried on Sunday 19th May. I went down the day previous and saw the remains at H. M. Eddison's, late that evening, her little curls looked so natural. W. E. Turner and Jno. Cowgill present. The day of the interment was very bright and Leeds looked almost inviting. Called on W. Cudworth before Meeting, cannot either read or write from giddiness in the head when so occupied. What a rich blessing is good health.

**22nd May** – Quite a winter's day with cold north wind and frequent storms of snow and hail. The nights of 23 and 24th were sharp frosts so that the potatoes are much injured by it etc. etc. Went to the Y.M. Slept one night at Cos. William's and called, Rebecca, Wm and I, upon Aunt Ann Shillitoe, found her apparently cheerful but often in great suffering.

**1st June** – Warm weather again, but I have no swarms, T. Latchmore has two from his hives exposed to the sun. Jno. & Anna came today from the Yearly Meeting. It being our first Saturday half holiday we made a party to Bendish, Joseph & Sarah Ann, Miss Harper, Jno. & Anna (after attending Yearly Meeting) Maria and Annie Latchmore from Leicester (who is expecting to sail for New Zealand with their family next week) Rebecca and myself. Had tea at the 'Harrows' and then walked to Titmus's Farm which is to be sold shortly. If the price is low enough perhaps I may be tempted to purchase. It is a pleasant situation but the land wants draining, etc.

WM: *Hives that are heated by the sun too much are more likely to throw swarms; colonies kept in shade under trees will swarm less.*

**7th June** – For days past it has been cool, windy showery weather so that the bees have made scarcely any progress – no swarms yet.

**10th June** – The first swarm. Put it into Rebecca's hive whose bees died in the winter. It being a swarm of last year the comb was good. Weather summer like at last. TL beginning to cut his hay. Warmer weather lasted but a few days for it was succeeded with very dull cloudy time with north and east wind till the 21st of June on which day Jno. Ransom was buried after being at Benslow exactly 12 years to the day. There was a very large funeral. Cos. William on a visit to us. A nice account read after tea at Benslow of JR's last suffering months drawn up by Jane Ransom. He had completed his 80 years last month.

WM: *Writers of the day recognised the importance of using fresh comb. If the comb was dark and had been used for several years of brood-rearing the risk of diseases (especially the foul-broods) would have been much greater.*

**26th June** – Cos. William on a week's visit. He was quietly walking in TL's garden when a bee darted at him and stung him on the face just below the eye. He gave a sharp cry. Tobacco water was applied after Rebecca had quickly pulled out the sting and either it or his good blood caused but little ill effect to show. William and I gathered a large basket full of Black Prince strawberries on Sunday afternoon. Bees gathering but little honey; nights and morning very cool.

WM: *When a bee stings the sting sac is usually left attached to the sting, with a muscle continuing to pump toxin even after the bee itself has broken away. Bee-keepers quickly learn that the effects of a bee sting can be reduced by scratching out the sting as quickly as possible.*
*Cousin William may well have had 'good blood'. Today we could explain this in terms of having blood proteins (immunoglobulins) that suppress the effects of the toxins.*

**30th June** – Sunday – The first chapter of Isaiah and 1st chapter of John read by J H Tuke at our morning meeting this day. Although some Friends had disapproved of the change all had acquiesced but Ann Leadbetter who remained prim to the last. How will it end?

**1st July** – Vines in flower and limes in some situations.

**3rd July** – To Bletsoe for J. S. Crawley's Rents, getting out at Sharnbrook Station. Suppose for the last time as Midland Railway will be open to Luton in a few months. Beautiful showers for two days succeeded by sunny weather.

**6th July** – Saturday – Arthur Latchmore being at home from Falmouth we, Arthur, Maria and Annie also Emma Kingsley and self had tea at the cottage at Lilly Hoo. I walked there by Smoothys and Wellbury and Little Offley. After tea went to the Hills. E.K. while attempting to skip down a little incline fell and bruised her shoulder – dear Rebecca started today for Chesterfield and some sea side place with Mary, etc.

**8th July** – Arthur Latchmore at home for a holiday. Got him to bottle some milk after scalding it, corking it tightly down; one of plain milk, one a little salt in it and the other carbonate of soda. The first opened at supper last evening the 10th. It proved very good and sweet, the others opened tonight. There was no sign of sourness whatsoever, but the milk was unpleasantly flavoured with the old corks used. AL and I went to Joseph's after supper and talked the matter over with them. Mrs Paul from London there. I proposed Arthur should prepare some milk tomorrow for them to try it and that Mrs P. should take some to London with her when she returns so that it might be proved after travelling and keeping in London a few days, which was agreed to. For genuine milk 6d per quart is charged. Joseph had said only today that next winter he would go to London and try and find some school customers for his skim milk, for the sake of the poor London children. I hope something will come of it.

**19th July** – The first flower show in connection with the School. Up at 5 o'clock and by working hard til 10 o'clock got a fine basket of flowers ready also three kinds of cherries, three currants, raspberries strawberries and four kinds of gooseberries. I was surprised to get the second prize for fruit and the third for flowers. The latter basket was made handsome with a large cluster of the bright rose from the orchard and French and common honeysuckle, particularly the former, while lilies and clarkia very effective mixed with blue branching larkspur and the evergreen barberries. Jos. Sharples allowed the company to walk in the plantation besides exhibiting many beautiful plants. It proved a very wet evening while at tea in the tent. The Meeting afterwards held in the barn. A deputation from Birmingham present. Jas. H. Tuke in the chair. The next day 7th day afternoon went with F. Seebohm and Jno. McCormack to Lilly Hoo – walking from Wellbury to the Hoo round the hills to Highdown and to tea at J. H. Tuke's at 7 o'clock with the Committee of Scholars – a very interesting time, J H Tuke closing with remarks on talents not employed. It was a seed sowing meeting; good fruit must result from it.

Roses grafted from Mount Pleasant:
No 1 Washington & Prince Camile de Rohen
No 2 ditto only the middle stem by the terrace
No 3 Souvenir de la Malmason & Washington
No 4 Julis Margitten & Anna de Diesbach

Also plum shoot from orchard near beech hedge and cherry grafted, May Duke

**24th July** – To Tottenham to Aunt Ann's funeral.

**26th July** – Pouring wet all day. It has been windy showery weather for about a fortnight – a very poor season for bees.

For our holiday this summer Rebecca went to Chesterfield and Bridlington with Mary and children, and I to Paris Exhibition with Arthur Willmore, Benwell and Joseph Latchmore via Newhaven & Dieppe, staying at Cook'st Hotel, Rue de la Faisanderie.

The swifts left about the usual time, the 18th of August, but one pair stayed till 8th September and one martin seen in November. Apples are a great failure this season. Plums plentiful and some kinds of pears. Potatoes in the orchard have turned out much better than many of our neighbours – in damp situations they are very bad.

Wm Impey gave me some strawberry plants set them in the orchard and Harper at the Engine House gave me some British Queens. Set them in Fishpond garden.

**30th October** – Mary Best staying with us. She planted this day a Hawthornden apple tree in the Bank Garden.

**11th November** – Planted potatoes today to see if they are better than those planted in the spring – using ashes, road scrapings.The Workman's Hall rising out of the ground. New public houses talked of in Brand Street belonging to Lucas C. and Jno Steed† – very annoying to the promoters of Workman's Hall, Joseph Sharples, J. H. Tuke, F Seebohm, and Alf. & W Ransom. – JS gives £1,000 to it.

**Joshua Whiting in old age**

# 1868

**31st January** – The winter so far has been wet and stormy but no very severe frost but very changeable. After snow had been on the ground some days and gone again I went into the garden and noticed some hives had the straws close by the entrance either nibbled by mice or pecked by birds, but the latter I believe as quantities of great tomtits were so often in the garden by the hives. So T. L. Frank and I set two rat traps and in a few days caught nine of them. I have long noticed their love for bees by the quantities of remains under the damson tree. I am sorry for their destruction but the bees must be protected. Chimonanthus in full flower.

**17th February** – A very fine February – the sunset tonight most beautiful. Rebecca sent flowers by packet post to Esther and Anna.

**21st February** – Saw farina taken in today. Another sunny day. Bees very busy and musical. John Steed brought last market day a large posy of single snowdrops from his wife, they are now on the table looking most fairy like. Last Sunday morning Ann Leadbetter (Martha Lucas's companion) gave us a short sermon on the "wanton destruction of the lower creation" quoting "the Lord's tender mercies are over all his works", etc. The destruction of tomtits being generally known among the Thompsons & Lucases etc. made some think it was an allusion to their destruction; others to foxes, as Clement Lucas is now confined to his bed with a broken leg done while hunting. All agree it was a <u>short</u> sermon that will be <u>long</u> remembered. One Friend thought of wasps and flies as the object of her appeal, a Gentleman Friend W. S. Read of her acquaintance being much in the habit of destroying all within his reach.

**16th March** – A very mild March so far wind mostly south west. Apricot almost over and *Pyrus Japonica* fully out growing at the foot of one of the elm trees.

**21st March** – Quite a warm growing day, wind still south. Daffodils out, and gooseberries also. In a letter from Thomas he says that Philip Slack brought him the other day a live drone. The earliest date they had known them out before was 5th May, 1865. I find Thos, Joseph and I saw drones in our "Folly hive" on Sunday the 9th of April, 1854 and I find that my memorandum says for that year that it was the best honey season for years past, perhaps these early drones prognosticate a similar one this year. I find also in 1857 drones were seen by us on 1st April. It was a very good season for honey and the best known for wheat for many years.

WM: *This entry is three years after the Great Exhibition in the Crystal Palace at Hyde Park in 1851. In that year John Milton published* Milton's Practical Bee-Keeper *and described the hives he exhibited there. One of these 'Milton's Mansion of Industry' may have been the inspiration for Joshua Whiting's 'folly hive'. The appearance of drones is a sign of the commencement of preparations for breeding, and normally indicates that the colony has survived the winter and is building strongly.*

**25th March** – A sharp frost of seven degrees – will the apricots and peaches suffer?

**28th March** – Blackthorn just out in the garden hedge and was the same date in 1863.

**4th April** – Almost a summer's day; went a ride to the Anemone Banks[27] (Saturday afternoon).

**10th April** – Good Friday – unlike many Good Fridays of late years this has been cold with slight fall of snow last night, so we have stayed at home. Called on Mary Burr in morning and I on Miss Palmer. To tea at Alf. Ransom's. Planted last autumn Catillac Pear for baking next to summer house and Beurre Berckmans near to it also next to the path and Jefferson Plum close to it. Ickworth Imperatice Plum next to asparagus bed and Superb adjoining – Coe's Golden Drop opposite. Several sharp frosts the last few nights plums and pears most kinds in full blossom.

**22nd April** – Some days of rain and very windy. Found Silcocks' hive that I had not fed many of the bees dead, and all could soon have died for want of food.

**29th April** – Swallows came about 10 days since. Blossom of all kinds very abundant. Often cold windy weather but so far only a few days from the east.

**4th May** – Hot sun with frost at nights and wind east. Swifts and drones just made their appearance.

**7th May** – Sent a box of tulips and asparagus to Thomas. Both have been given away freely by Rebecca to our friends.

**25th May** – A dry May till the 23rd and 24th – no swarms for either TL or myself, but some in the villages by the beginning of the month. Ellen with us 1st day, middle of Yearly Meeting. I went at beginning – Josiah Foster strongly disapproved of Bible being read in Meeting. Said he could not conscientiously attend where such was the case. Much difference of opinion on various subjects. [*next sentence heavily crossed out*].

**24th May** – Found Ellen three Black Prince strawberries nearly ripe. The season very early.

**27th May** – The first swarm Re's, which she sold to TL to take to neighbours for 10s.

WM:   *It would seem that bees as well as honey were being sold to Neighbour & Son.*

**28th May** – Another swarm joined with two of TL's. The next day they all came out again they were not shaded from the sun – an unusually dry May. Stacks quite heavy.

**20th June** – No rain worth mentioning to date, with sunshine continually so that every thing is very dry. Honey very plentiful, as usual in such seasons. Had my holiday the first part of this month.

The first three days out with John and Anna, Joseph driving us to St Albans. Went over the Abbey then by rail to Rickmansworth;

called to see W. Penn's house, but told it had been rebuilt. Then drove to Chenies. Found a good inn and beautiful village and park of Lord Chesham's. The Glasiers of Leyton staying like us for the night on our way to Jordans. The Bedford family are buried in the church – many monuments to them. Started early next morning for Jordans Monthly Meeting, the road very winding and most part the lanes very beautiful. On arriving at Chalfont St Giles drove to the Post Office expecting to find my friend W. Goodman but he had moved to Botterills Farm a mile distant, where Isaac Penington had lived, also Thos Ellwood as tutor. Some parts of the house appear the same as when they lived there. Then to Jordans by way of "3 Households".

Morning dull and some very fine rain when in Meeting that added to the beauty of the lime trees that were so conspicuous as I sat in Meeting. A crowded house gathered, as Christine Alsop† said in her opening sermon, from the north, south, east and west. Amos and Edith Griffith also, from America; the Lady a pleasant speaker. Her husband a <u>very quiet</u> man. Cranstone of Hemel Hempstead invited me to share their dinner under the trees. Afterwards, examined the first visitor's autograph book placed there by Phebe Allen when they lived at Amersham. Left early for our long ride to Berkhampstead. Not so comfortable as Chenies in every respect, quite to Anna's annoyance. Started next morning for Aldbury at the foot of the Hill by the monument in Ashridge Park. Had a beautiful walk about it, large herds of deer but the beech trees were John's great admiration. Continued our walk over the downs to Dunstable, resting on the top under the shade of a tree.

On morning of 7th June, John, Anna, Cos. William, Rebecca and I all started by third class train for Leeds – a very cheerful ride. Edward Latchmore to meet us at the station and a warm reception at Ridgmont from Esther and Etty and Mary. A game at croquet in the evening. Weather quite cold, a good fire at breakfast time and going over the moor to Meeting morning and evening was like Christmas. Monday – to the exhibition in the new Infirmary.28 Tuesday – Edward and Esther and Etty and Mary with Cos. William Rebecca and self all started for a four day excursion first to Ilkley and then by car to Bolton stopping at Farmer Ellis's. Warm welcome, fine oak wainscoting up stairs. To Red Lion at Bolton. Drove to Barden Tower and returned opposite side of the river. In the evening, Edward, William & I strolled about the Abbey & on the high ground opposite, returning home by the Terrace – a beautiful evening. Next morning drove to Barden Tower & all lingered long in the beautiful fern covered [space here]. Mary Latchmore was almost wild with delight, & Cos William & Rebecca & I got a quantity to bring home; William making his up into a bundle that we called his Baby from Barden. A fine drive with Appletreewick (where old Mrs Winterburne came from) in the Valley below. Stopped at Grassington while Edward paid for their hams obtained at a customer's. While getting over the narrow fall of water, William nearly slipped into the very deep hole.

Edward, Wm & I parted with the ladies & walked beside the river (starting up a heron) on to Buckden – had to sleep there, & next morning started in two country conveyances for Leyburn going through Bishopsdale & part of Wensleydale. Bolton Castle in view – had a beautiful walk on the shawl[29] at Leyburn – extensive prospect up Wensleydale etc. The next day drove to Pateley Bridge by Fountains Abbey – a large ruin – fine drive over the moors & deep descent into Pateley.

**23rd June** – Took from a hive that had not swarmed a topping weighing 24lbs. TL sold it to neighbours at 1s 3d – £1. 6s net. A little rain the other day. Wheat as usual in dry summers looking remarkably well. Grapes quite a size. Lime blossoms beginning to fall on some trees.

**24th June** – Drove with J H Tuke to Ampthill preparing for balance. In many places the blackberry out in full blossom.

**8th July** – Hot dry weather still continues – potatoes very small.

**13th July** – Wheat cutting generally begun about us, crops of wheat very fine and not laid at all, late sown barley etc. very middling – straw very short – no turnips worth mentioning or second crops of hay. A shower yesterday the first for a long time.

**15th July** – "St Swithin's". The hottest day for many years.

**22nd July** – Each day is hotter than the previous. Thermometer in the shade at Theodore Lucas's today at 88; often appearances of rain but none comes to us. The prospect of potatoes very bad, excepting the early ones.

**23rd July** – A very great change today being 23 degrees less than yesterday, wind north. Went to Ampthill by train via Bedford for the first time. Carting of wheat, etc general.

**27th July** – T B Smithies, editor of 'British Workman' came on Saturday evening and stayed till Monday. Addressed both Girls' and Boys' School from the 1st Psalm – particularly from the words in first verse: walketh, standeth and sitteth.

**1st August** – Almost uninterrupted sunshine so few clouds and yet but very little dew. The barley so dry that with difficulty it is kept on the carts. Half the grass in the park was burnt yesterday. Rebecca & I walked across it in the evening. It reminded me of a black Yorkshire moor. Milk risen to 7d per quart and butter 1s 8d per lb.

**7th August** – Woken this morning by the beautiful sound of falling rain but it was only a shower. Alfred Ransom finished his harvest this year the same day of the month that he began it last year.

**9th August** – Helen Gilpin† is on a visit at W Ransom before going to Madagascar – spent most of the day with us – called on Mary Burr as we returned from the School – she is a lively Christian. The Sewells to tea.

**15th August** – To Baldock. M. A. Steed's funeral, large flocks of crows and starlings near the town flying as in autumn. TL drove Rebecca and I. Went to the ground before going to the house. The surroundings of the grave very different to ours. A large heap of chalk to one side of it – saw that the Meeting House was opened and ventilated. Edward and Caroline May spoke at the grave and in Meeting also, Alf Ransom and Rebecca in Meeting as well. J & E Sharples, Ed. Sewell, J. Thompson, W. Ransom and Maria Feltham also present.

**21st August** – Theodore Lucas informs me that the amount of rain that fell in May 0.57, June 0.42 and July 0.24 made a total for 3 months of 1.23, but for the last fortnight we have had occasional showers, the last one a very heavy fall of 1½ inches in 3 hours being more than we had in the three months as above. The grass is now growing most rapidly and our park that was so black after the burning of the dried grass is now as green as possible and is preferred by the sheep to that which was not burned.

**September** – The whole of this month we have been at Ampthill, very hot, when we went the driver said the sun's heat was more like July than September, very cold a few days after wards with an east wind. The chestnuts very abundant and ripe in the park, trees very little changing their foliage, heath mostly dried up. Had a pleasant evening with old Scott, the Beemaster at Steppingley. He has bought a few more stocks and now has 70 hives of bees. His grapes are very fine, he brought us some of the finest bunches for a present. George Allen showed me how to distinguish the champinions, an edible funghi, which some think superior to mushrooms; we have had some, and like them. The meeting is smaller than ever, Edward White walks over to Aspley every first day morning to the Meeting there, and Thomas Corder does not come. Mary White is more infirm, her legs are weak, Maria Brown and James Matthews better than two years ago. Ann Brown at home having left Ackworth; [30] teaching the tenth class, too much for her. Jemima Richardson, the Hagen's servant, is an original. We are often amused at her sayings and doings, she is very deaf. Harry Wildman, grown, he is now 14. "Soft Sam" pumps water and cleans knives and boots, as before – this year there is a large cat, a kind of Persian, as well as the old one, and for a wonder, no kittens. The Hagens and their adopted daughter Lizzie Bramly, are gone to Leicester. Rebecca came with me and returned with the conveyance, as Fred Marsh was away at Luton, she came to stay on my birthday, 48, and brought me the present of a pair of slippers, also a plum pudding for dinner. Frank Latchmore drove Rebecca and Maria over and before that day next week, Frank was on his voyage to New Zealand, he <u>intends</u> being a sheep farmer there. They had some rough weather in the Channel, lost an anchor near the Goodwin Sands and were much tossed about. Maria and Lucy Sewell commenced their school for little boys at the Workman's Hall. They began with five.

The contracts for our house in the Bedford Road are out. I went over to Hitchin on Saturday to see Mr Shilcock the Architect, about a few alterations in the plans. I have accepted George Jeeves's tender, he was the lowest, though all five were nearly alike. Seymour is the carpenter. A notice of it was inserted in *The Builder*.[31] Poor Rebecca had not been at Ampthill many days before she had an attack of spasmodic sciatica, and was very ill, we had to call in a Dr Evershed. The Friends were all very kind doing what they could for us. May and Ann Brown nursed Rebecca. Geo Allen kind in sending a fowl and apples. We were glad when 5th of October came for us to return home. Our house was begun that morning. The well was only about 17 feet when water came principally through soft chalk. Some is kept for garden paths – only a mixture of chalk and earth found in the cellar. The first woodwork appeared and the door frame of wine cellar and stone steps of ditto at same time.

**17th October** – The foundations and cellar walls are just above the ground at the end of a fortnight. Next week more bricklayers are coming so that another fortnight will make greater progress. Brother Thomas and Cos. William with us last week. Principally at their suggestion gave up the earth closets as substitute for water closet after taking much pains to adopt the earth closet but conclude to have one for servants' use out of the back kitchen. Beautiful weather so far for building.

**20th October** –Market Day. By gas light[32] found some progress had been made since the morning. The large door stone of drawing room window put in its place and the first door posts fixed in scullery.

**26th October** – Part of two days last week were very wet but still good progress has been made. The front door posts put up today and some white bricks built up to them. Clark & Chalkley busy laying out part of the path next to the wall. Decided to have it four feet wide and box for edging. Chalk dug out of the well at the bottom then cinders from Jno. Gatward's foundry.

**29th October** – Saml. Allen buried this day – would have been 97 the 15th of next month. Robt. and Christine Alsop the only speakers at the grave and Meeting. The robin as usual sang while we were standing round the grave. R. Alsop's text was "the work of righteousness is peace", etc.

**30th October** – A week of fine weather. The house progresses rapidly nearly up to the first storey and the rooms now begin to show what size they will be. The kitchen appears rather narrow – had the scullery window taken out – it was so small and a good size one substituted. The four foot garden path completed excepting gravel and evergreen plants. Pear, apple and plum trees moved to middle of garden and pampas grass brought down from the orchard. A wonderful year for acorns, used for sheep and pigs. Turnips, etc. very poor after the hot summer.

**21st November** – The house will be ready for the roof on the 23rd. The weather up to this time having been very favourable only a few showers and occasional frosts. Clark and Chalkley made the rockwork today took two loads of Jeeves's clinkers, planted in the centre a weeping American willow and one each side a Balm of Gilead fir. It is a great addition to the garden, and if the trees grow they will make a nice blind to Mrs Squire's and Joseph White's cottages.

Brother Joseph planted this week over 300 plum trees in Benj. Tatham's old field. Clark planted them. Thomas here yesterday, voting for Cowper and Brand. Had the morning from the Bank, called on Abby, Miss Wilsher's old servant and on to Bedford Road and the plum orchard. How will it look in seven years time?

**5th December** – The carpenters have been engaged upon the roof for ten days and now it is partly slated. Showery and windy. We have often wished more expedition had been made while the fine weather lasted. Painters and plumbers at work (R & T Newton). Planting an edging of thrift in the orchard. Rebecca divided the large roots, hope it may grow as many pieces had no roots to begin with.

**14th December** – The roof finished slating today, from various causes it has been a long time about.

Mrs Robinson much frightened the other night by the wind blowing off slates through her bedroom window and the rain came through Day's ceiling for some hours, but both took it good naturedly. But very little frost so far, but often high winds and showery. Cows still go to Butts Close and common – a very unusual thing. The remainder of December wet and windy. Cos. William spent Xmas with us. Walked to Charlton, calling on the old Morgans – their cottage gay with jessamine and sun shining in – old man very deaf.

# 1869

**9th January** – No frost yet and today very mild. Birds singing like spring time. Rebecca gathered nine kinds of flowers, making a very pretty basket with small ivy leaves round.

**20th January** – A "Bee";[33] about 20 attending to work at Helen Gilpin's outfit for Madagascar. Letters from Jos. Sewell and Sarah Street read, also from Sister Mary from Corsica, and one from Thomas with an account of Aunt Heppenstall's funeral. Amos and Edith Griffith present. They well remembered grandfather[34] when he was in America being at their house. Weather continues almost without frost.

**23 & 24th January** – Eight degrees of frost for about two days and then mild weather again.

**28th January** – Elizth. Tuke buried today. The morning promised to be wet but about noon it cleared up to be a sunny warm afternoon, the lark singing high up while the large company were standing round the grave. A few days after it was planted round with crocuses and violets. JH Tuke appears with crêpe in his hat and children all in black.[35]

**11th February** – Very mild weather continues. At the Bible reading Meeting the other day at our house Rebecca had got a beautiful dish of flowers, three kinds of crocuses, squill, Virginia stock, violets, snowdrops, anemones, primrose, *Pyrus japonica*. Clark sowed 5 lb grass seed at the back of new house and a gentle rain succeeded, so trust it may grow. Some of the apricot blossom out, and blackthorn.

Purchased in London yesterday *Lilium Excelsiu*m said to be lemon colour and sweet scented.

**15th February** – Carpenters taken possession of the house today and commenced with putting down cellar steps. Bricklayers building the pillars for the side gate. Sparrows troublesome at the grass seed. Cotton with feathers and scarlet flannel tied to it do not keep them away. Continued mild weather a beautiful nosegay of *Pyrus japonica* and *Laurustinus*.

**5th March** – The <u>bricklayers</u> have finished this evening. Just five months they have been at work. Carpenters and painters still to complete. A cundys ? stove in the kitchen added a warm air chamber to it. Hope the whole affair will settle well. It has been a source of many cogitations. Drying winds just now. Advertised in *The Friend*, but no applications at present.

**19th March** – Rebecca and I went to see Helen Gilpin off by the train for Liverpool expecting to leave for Madagascar 10th of April. All think her very suitable. She reminded us much of Sister Anna.

March up to yesterday has been very cold – more frost than last month.

**26th March** – Good Friday – A change in the wind yesterday and today as usual the sun has shone out, the bees especially rejoicing in the change. Rebecca and I after spending some time at the house lighting the drawing room fire etc, walked to Ickleford to call on Thos. Priest and see over his new house. Found him in bed. His anemone and single daffodils very gay. Thos. Morris from Royston saw us in the garden and went thro' Taylor's garden by Rowley's Mill. Chalkley putting on the fine gravel today, glad to see the grass seeds coming up.

**10th April** – Rebecca planted an acorn in the garden today that she has grown on the mantle piece all the winter. Helen Gilpin sails for Madagascar today. Jno. and Anna and W. Ransom see her off. Mary and Edith and Emily have been spending a fortnight with us leaving this morning after a pleasant visit, although the weather has been cold most of the time. The very early spring that February promised us has not been realized. Plum blossom and blackthorn being only now fully out. The greengage in the Bank garden never had so much blossom before.

**28th April** – Fras. Lucas said he saw swifts today – beautiful weather of late. Amos & Edith Griffith from America who well remember grandfather, here on Sunday – went with Amos to Highbury – both at Aunt Heppenstall's funeral.

**16th May** – Sunday before Yearly Meeting, Isaac and Sarah Robson, John Ford, Elizth. Hopkins and other strangers. Elzth. Sharples in a very critical state – died 19th May aged 78.

A very different May to last year – plenty of showers. Gathered a wild rose at Ippollitts.

**23rd May** – My first swarm. TL took to London. Frank Warner left us for Hertford Bank. Sorry to part with him, Herbert Clarke of Chatteris came today.

Planted *Solanum Giganteum* (by *Chimenanthus Fragrans*) a native of Australia. Showery and cool weather till 1st June. Edward and Esther came to Joseph's after YM. Etty and Mary and Eliza Latchmore to TL's and Cos. Ann and sister Anna to us. Arthur also from Falmouth.

**11th June** – A fine week for the hay. Etty and Mary have much enjoyed hay making – a good photo taken by [George] Avery†. Ben said he could not do it, little thinking his opponent would be employed. Purchased a copy – Miss Bless, Bob & Ellen came today.

**21st June** – Very cool showery weather for ten days past, a fire in the Bank today and several days this month and in parlour also – a very poor prospect for honey.

**1st July** – A continuance of cold cloudy weather with north east wind – only three swarms out of eight stocks and no casts. Vines not yet in flower.

**3rd July** – The sun again came out after nearly a week's absence.

**7th July** – The Flower Show – A very beautiful day and large attendance. Fourth prize for fruit. First time prizes given to the women for home made bread. Rebecca made both white and brown but not for competition; it was highly commended. Geo Canley [?] Mr Drake's man, 'The Author', gave Rebecca his prize wild flowers for selling his books.

**10th July** – Vine in full flower.

**24th July** – Thomas has been with us for a week and William at Joseph's. Jno. Best came unexpectedly the same evening so T. got him a bed at The Cock. Weather very dry and warm, but not a good honey. Seaton, TL, Thomas, William and I drove to Guilden Morden to call on Pierce and see his bees and then to Ashwell to Thorn's who has built a house on purpose for them. All his are on the Woodbury system – we all very much enjoyed the out. Thomas took Gyp Harlow back to Sheffield, and an eke of honey of course. Our yucca at last in flower – after being planted in 1861. The spike of flowers is four ft long – glad it was out when Thomas and William were here as our garden is rather bare of flowers.

WM:  *In this country there has never been a strong tradition of keeping bees in bee-houses. With the increased mobility of an affluent nation, more bee-keepers would have been made familiar with the bee-house tradition of south-eastern Europe. It is a logical solution to protecting hives of any sort from the extremes of weather, so will be "invented" anew from time to time.*
*Thomas White Woodbury (1818-1870) lived in Devon from the age of 14 years, and retired early from journalism on health grounds about 1850. He published numerous items on bee-keeping and corresponded with Darwin, Langstroth and others. Following the development of the moveable frame hive by Langstroth, Woodbury introduced his 10-frame moveable frame hive made of inch thick pine.*

**3rd August** – Only once rain last month for a few hours and again today.

**4th August** – Frank Latchmore left for Canada this morning – dull at leaving Benwell, went with him to Liverpool.

**14th August** – Robt Jackson came past to consult about Chesterfield affairs. Went with him to the station and saw waiting a hearse and found, as I expected, it was for W. Ransom's bright little

Maggie – while enlarging his house the family went to Birmingham all as well as usual. It is supposed M died from effects of a fall which injured the spine – <u>all</u> returned home together, but how changed!

**22nd August** – Gathered a basket of greengage plums at the Bank. Last year's hot summer I suppose suited it as it never had anything like the quantity before – will it be our <u>last</u> gathering of them? Ladybirds <u>very</u> plentiful all over the country – on the roads and fields. Insect blights have done much damage to many things. The main body of the swifts took their departure 18th, but this evening (23rd) saw one was left and doubtless there are more.

**25th August** – Rebecca and I started for Ipswich by boat from London Bridge with fine weather and slept at Woodbridge. Called upon Mark & Peter Buckmaster who lived near B. Barton's† little house in a corner of their street. Next morning on to Aldbro' found comfortable lodgings at Mr Newby's, Ironmonger. After two hot days Sunday was very cold and stormy – the change enabled me to take long walks to Orford and returned by boat to Orford and dog cart to Woodbridge – called on J. J. Neaves' father and mother and had tea at the Meeting House. Slept at Millicent Breverton's at Ipswich, and by steamer the next day for London.

**9th September** – Scarcely any rain for weeks past. The apples are <u>very</u> maggoty, plums plentiful.

**15th September** – Flower Show today – May, Ellen and E Sedgwick with us – helped in getting ready fruit and flowers and were delighted on finding I had first prize for fruit. It was much to my surprise, but our grapes were for the season very good. If we are living at Bedford Road next autumn shall not expect a prize as we shall not have the Bank garden and Fishponds to gather from.

**25th September** – Herbert E. Clarke of Chatteris left us and the Bank after being four months – he proved disagreeable in so many ways that we decided to leave the Bank house supposing that <u>he</u> was going to remain.

**27th September** – Jno. T. Warner came for a week, a very pleasant contrast, much like his brother Frank.

**2nd October** – Mary E. and E. Sedgwick with Rebecca & I had tea in the drawing room, M & E fetching it from the Bank – stayed till it was dusk. Rebecca's birthday.

The worst season for apples known for many years.

**4th October** – Wm Tindall Lucas came to the Bank today. On the 9th May, Ellen & Emily and I walked to Jas. Lucas's. Emily gave him a pot of blackberry jam and in return she had a good supply of toffee drops and 6d, which E. talks of keeping. Warm sunny weather – our grapes good. Mr Tuck of Wymondley said he never knew a year when he was better repaid for thinning of some of his – a present from W. Ransom of two bunches of his Hambro' in return for a like instruction. I have his man in, thinning out the bunches.

**29th November** – For a month past, I have been busy removing trees and plants of all sorts from our old garden to the new house as we decided to leave the Bank. Bees of course are removed also. Planted three grape vines, Early Frontignan near the drawing room door, Early Malrasen at back of coal place and back of tool place.

# 1870

**25th February** – A very good deal of frost this winter with cold east winds. We leave the old Bank house for Bedford Road the 9th of next month. Busy papering, but Rebecca prisoner indoors for weeks past – much wants to see how the house is getting on. Find two stocks of bees dead, the remainder very light.

**3rd March** – Settled today with J. H. Tuke about the fixtures we have put up at the Bank, he & F. Seebohm went all over the house. I received £20 for them. Tomorrow Langford's men[36] commence with taking up the drawing room carpet. Removing accomplished comfortably – fine weather all the time. Rebecca made use of Jno. Bent's fly to bring up many things. The whole of March very cold except for about four days, with frosty nights so that now, on 6th April, peaches only just coming out. Apricots look very bad, no pear or plum blossom to be seen.

**13th April** – Good Friday – A fine sunny day as usual. Geo Knight came to breakfast and I put together a strong Jonah's Broth. Rebecca planting nasturtiums etc. I was in the garden all the day till we went to tea at TL's to meet Geo & Emma. The next day Arthur Willmore brought Emily Ann Wolf, driving from Woburn here by half past nine – had her photo taken by Ben. We were pleased with her – sat in the booth in the afternoon and watched the tortoise[37] go into his home at 4 o'clock as Gilbert White describes his as doing. She left after tea.

**15th April** – Saw the first swallow and queen wasp in the orchard also the wryneck.

**21st June** – A remarkable dry spring. TL has not half his usual crop of hay and in many places the grass is not worth cutting. The season is much like 1863.

**6th July** – F. L. Latchmore returned from Canada. The first six months of this year are the driest that the Lucas's have recorded during the time of their taking note of rainfalls.

**22 August** – The memorable dry summer of 1870 has broken up today. We have only had occasional slight showers since February. Pastures entirely brown and bare. Harvest generally completed. Wheat of course first rate. Our peaches and apricots have been very plentiful and plums – Coe's Golden Drop – an enormous crop.

Went for our holiday to Whitby staying at Sheffield going and Chesterfield returning. Thomas's garden the admiration of all passers by, grass so trim and green – but his flowers are readily stolen – he will not grow them again. On Sunday afternoon he was greatly employed in keeping out boys from pursuing butterflies over his beds. I made an excursion to Ayton School,[38] much pleased. Stayed at the boarding house. The Wells from America, and May, daughter of Isaac Sharp [the elder]†, and the widow of a French man with May Weatheral for housekeeper. The children had not returned. Cleveland Lodge the residence of late Jno. Pease – very pleasantly situated with fine hill in the distance – went over the house and gardens. The gardener told me that Malmaison Rose strikes good by cuttings put in ground in October. May Sedgwicks and E & E with us for a week – lodged at M. Robinson's, Cliff Street.

WM:   *As so often seems to happen, after a good honey year there follow the bad. Joshua says nothing of taking honey from his stocks. If this means he took none, this is just as well. We can see that this was the middle of at least four years of indifferent weather for the bees. Are we seeing a decline in interest as a result of this, or are there other factors that explain the diminishing record of Joshua and Re's bee-keeping?*

**10th September** – My fiftieth birthday – can it be possible? – dearest Rebecca read me letters she had received against the day as soon as I awoke, from Thomas, Mary, and Cos. William. She had received them unknown to me the day before – her present was a pocket hand-

**J. Sharples and his wife**

kerchief beautifully marked, but she found in doing it that her eyesight like mine does not improve. How much I should do that I have not done & leave undone that that I have done! If it was possible to live life over again – May the remembrance of these regrets be of use for the remaining fraction of my life. But we have not a hard Master, but one that has carried our sorrows & been tempted in all points like we are.

The second post brought letters from Esther & May Latchmore & Mary Sedgwick & Ellen Jackson. Thos. Latchmore also sent me a note & garden clippers – Emma Kingsley a pork pie of her own make and Jane Ransom called with grapes from Joseph Sharples, but not knowing it was my birthday – all the better pleased to find it so. My dearest Rebecca & I planted narcissus, crocus & anemone. Rests after dinner, as it was on a 7th day. Thos, Annie, Benwell & Maria came to tea and Jno. E. Whiting from Leeds also with us. My crowning mercy is in having the best of all wives. The morning of the day and night previous was extremely windy – blowing off nearly all our pears and apples. And a nice letter from Meta came a few days afterwards. Very little rain this month but very misty mornings and hot sunshine following.

**2nd October** – Re's birthday – 43 – Sunday. Drove to Baldock – warm sunny day – in Joseph's wicker chaise – returned as usual by Willian. Six at Meeting, Jno. Steed, and Oliver, his wife, and her sisters and us – an earnest prayer from dear Rebecca – followed by a practical discourse on the 27th psalm, particularly on the first and third verse.

SG: *The first and third verse of Psalm 27: "The land is my light and my salvation; whom shall I fear? the Lord is the strength of my life; of whom shall I be afraid."*

**J. Sharples skating**

*"Though an host should encamp against me, my heart shall not fear: though war should rise against me, in this will I be confident."*

**28th October** – Isaac Brown† presented this evening at the Workman's Hall by 35 of his old Hitchin scholars with £500 and gold watch and photo album. A. Ransom and W. Westlake the chief promoters.

**29th October** – Most of the party set off to Barton Hills but it proved a very wet day – a large party at J. H. Tuke's in the evening – Mary stayed over Sunday and tea at J. Sharples' on Monday evening. May good results flow from it.

# 1871

Very sharp frost set in about 21st December and continued till about middle of January 1871 killing all broccoli and annuals and cutting down roses. There was skating on Jos. Sharples' plantation for a farthing bit; F. Seebohm, Theodore Lucas, Jno. Widdows, Jno. Warner, J. A. Sheppard and I, skated there before 10 o'clock. J. Sharples' skating days are over.

**1st March** – Still an absence of much rain to make up for last year's deficiency. Seven hives stood the winter, one died which a mouse took possession of and ate up some of the honey, but fortunately I discovered him early.

**22nd March** – Apricot blossom fully out. Jno. and Anna with us after attending farewell Meeting in London on Hy. Clark and W. Johnson's going to Madagascar. Lucy Sewell engaged to WJ. We walked to Maydencroft and on to Preston wood for violets, but did not find many wild ones, much to Anna's disappointment. Maria also went with us.

**25th March** – The weather warm and sunny that we have not required a fire all day. Peach blossom out.

**26th March** – 1st day – Another warm day – more like summer. Saw a large cobweb before breakfast and numbers of butterflies during the day – no fire all day again.

**4th April** – Good Friday – Seven degrees of frost last night covered one peach and apricot tree. Rebecca at Chesterfield with Annie Latchmore so started by the 5.08 train for Stevenage and walked to Fairlane farm and on to W. Heathcote's at Shephall Bury – beautiful new house, and back by Stevenage and called on Bank business on Mad Lucas.† Bright sun all day with cold easterly wind.

**8th April** – Another seven degrees of frost last night. Peach blossom past its best.

**9th April** – Eight degrees of frost – blackthorn generally out.

**20th April** – After very dry weather real April showers for three days past – a great relief to farmers as there is scarcely any hay left in this part.

**5th May** – Sister Mary came for the day before starting next week with Edward for the Continent. Richard Shillitoe came to tea, he has not long returned from China – a beautiful warm day after the cold and wet we have had for a fortnight.

**6th May** – Saw one swift today.

Most of May and up to 10th June very dry and often very cold. Edward & Esther staying with us after the Y. Meeting. Had a fire all day and sat round it at night like Christmas. They stayed over B. Seebohm's† funeral – a very large company from all parts of England. Richard Lamb from Sibford with others spoke at the grave. Did not go to the Meeting as D. Lloyd wished to go.

**12th June** – My first swarm or rather I believe three went together. Used a straw hive and Thomas's bar hive – placed them in a newly painted white shed that Thomas sent me after he gave up keeping bees. (This year one of the worst honey seasons I remember.)

**17th June** – John and Anna and Annie and Willie came today. Annie is very unexpectedly going with R. & C. Alsop to France – may be away four months. During the whole of the late wars, Annie always most warmly took the part of the French little thinking the part that is in prospect of endeavouring to raise their condition in some small degree.

**19th June** – Continued showery weather for ten days and very warm with it, so that every thing grows rapidly. Joseph's hay cut. It seems as though it would be quite spoilt. A great deal of blight particularly with currant trees. The old ones killed by it. An exceedingly small apple crop – but our pears plentiful. Winter Nelis bore largely – but no Maria Louise as the weather was so frosty when that tender pear was in flower. Sharp early frosts in November so that the chrysanthemums were spoilt. December wet and foggy. Joseph Sharples died this year – everything sold by auction at the house.

**Barn by Samuel Lucas**

# 1872

**31st January** – The whole of January continued wet and damp till today which has been beautiful – a large bat out this evening.

**8th February** – The same kind of weather and often warm with it – had the bank door open all the afternoon today. Aconites, snowdrops and violets out as the month came in and jessamine very beautiful all down our road.

**15th March** – Mild and damp till about this time then a week of frost and a heavy snow about 22nd March.

**19th April** – Sharp frost of seven degrees and 21st April – snow and hail.

**9th June** – The effect of the last entry has been that there is an almost total failure of plums and pears. Apples on some trees promise a fair crop. The weather has been very showery and cold. Lost one hive and great numbers from the others for want of food principally so that I have no swarms yet.

Fruit of 1872 was a complete failure. Apples selling at 10 to 12 shillings a bushel.

# 1873

Very wet autumn of 1872 and winter of 1873. Much snow in February and a very favourable late spring for the fruit.

**12th May** – Saw the first swifts and drones today. May came in very fine. Walked after tea with J. A. Sheppard and Algernon Warner to Bunyan's Dell – calling at the cottage.

[the last entry in the diary. Joshua's beloved Rebecca died in 1886].

\* \* \* \*

# *Envoi*

Mary Sturge Whiting (*right*) and Anna Maria (Whiting) Harvey (*left*), who were frequent visitors to Hitchin in their youth and who link their uncle, Joshua Whiting, with their great-niece and grand-daughter, Sarah Graham.

# *Some slants on history*

History is the essence of innumerable biographies.
Thomas Carlyle
*Critical and Miscellaneous Essays*: 'On History' 1838

There is no life of a man, faithfully recorded, but is a heroic poem of its sort, rhymed or unrhymed.
Thomas Carlyle
Essay on Walter Scott 1838

If we had a keen vision of all that is ordinary in human life, it would be like hearing the grass grow or the squirrel's heartbeat, and we should die of that roar, which is the other side of silence.
George Eliot
*Middlemarch* 1871

We are all the vehicles in which our ancestors ride.
Oliver Wendell Holmes

And that things are no so ill with you and me as they might have been, is half owing to the number who lived faithfully a hidden life.
George Eliot
*Middlemarch* 1871

# *Around the world 1861-1871*

1861    Outbreak of American Civil War
Serfdom abolished in Russia
Italy an independent kingdom

1862    Bismarck becomes Prussian premier

1863    Start of the world's first underground railway in London

1864    International Red Cross founded
International Working Men's Association in London
Construction of torpedo

1865    Assassination of Abraham Lincoln
End of American Civil War. American slaves freed.
Lister's antiseptic in use
First carpet-sweeper

1866    Nobel invents dynamite

1867    Fenian uprisings in Ireland and England
Bicycles manufactured in France
Garibaldi marches on Rome and is defeated

1868    Liberal revolution against Queen Isabella of Spain
Liberal victory over Conservatives in British general election

1869    Opening of Suez Canal
Launching of the Cutty Sark
Invention of celluloid, margarine and ball bearings.

1870    France defeated in Franco-Prussian War
Diamond mining in South Africa
Britain produced half the world's steel production.
71% of shipping using Suez Canal was British

1871    Paris Commune
Meeting of Stanley and Livingstone in East Africa

Dates taken from *Encyclopaedia of Dates*, editor Brian Phythian.
Hodder & Stoughton 1990.

# Some biographical sketches
# and personal references

## Samuel Allen

### 1771-1868

Samuel Allen came of strong Quaker stock (his brother, William Allen, pharmacist of Plough Court, joined with cousins to establish the firm of Allen & Hanbury). His marriage to Phebe Lucas brought him to Hitchin, where he lived from 1807 until his death. It was a long and happy marriage. Phebe, a renowned Hitchin belle, had reputedly turned down seventeen suitors before accepting Samuel's offer and she remained gay and outgoing in spite of her husband's noted gloom, which deepened into depression after her death. It is clear from Joshua's diary that Samuel and Phebe had at one time lived in Amersham and attended Jordans Meeting, but there is no clue as to what Samuel was doing or had done (before his marriage he had been a miller, in partnership with Robert Marriage of Maldon, Essex). It is quite possible that by his mid-thirties he had made or had inherited enough money to retire (as 'Samuel Allen, esq., of West Hill') and serve his Meeting and the surrounding clusters of Meetings in the travelling ministry.

# Robert and Christine (Majolier) Alsop
## 1803 – 1876 & 1805 – 1879

The Alsops were in the long established and still continuing tradition of Quaker marriages in which husband and wife worked closely together with an impressive sense of unity and shared support. Like the Whitings, they married late and were childless, but their circumstances gave them greater freedom. Robert had been successful in business and was able to retire in his forties (a remarkably frequent option for nineteenth century Quakers) and was ready to direct his energies to anti-slavery, temperance and education. Perhaps the focus of the Alsops' concern was determined by Christine, a charismatic and cultivated French woman, for they travelled and ministered widely in Europe and are best remembered for their courage and persistence in personal relief work in Paris during the aftermath of the Franco-Prussian war. It is said that more lives were lost in Paris during the Commune than in the French Revolution. Famine and violence were rife and Hitchin Friends may have been some of the first to hear details because James H. Tuke, within days of the German evacuation in March, 1871, was in Paris handing out bread and blankets supplied by Quaker funds.

Christine Alsop appealed to Yearly Meeting, urging prayerful concern for her countrymen. Three tracts were prepared and the Alsops set out, accompanied by two young Quakeresses. Joshua's niece, Anna (always Annie), my grandmother, was one of these. Very possibly she had heard from Hitchin of the dire situation, and with the support of remarkable parents, offered herself for service. In 1990 the *Friends Quarterly* published an article by my cousin Mary Rowlands, another grandchild of Annie's, entitled 'Please send my buff piqué.' It is a fascinating account, drawn from letters and journal notes, and I cannot resist adding that Annie received her dress from Leeds within a few days.

# Isaac Brown
## 1803-1895

The son of Quaker parents and educated at Quaker schools, he turned down the valuable offer of a clerkship with Overend Gurney in favour of a teaching career. The success of his school in Hitchin was evidence of his great ability and commitment. He was a fine classical scholar and an outstanding botanist. As a young man he had gone through a tough period of spiritual doubt and emerged gradually "into the light of belief in Christ," being remembered as "very gentle with the dull and ignorant" and "helpful to those discouraged by doubts and difficulties". After sixteen years, in 1845, the flourishing little Quaker Academy was destroyed by fire. No lives were lost, but it was impossible to rebuild. Isaac Brown left Hitchin with his family and became the first principal of the Flounders Institute at Ackworth, where twenty young men were to be trained as teachers in Quaker Schools. His zeal was such that, now in his forties, he studied at University College, London, attending classes in the classics, Hebrew and the sciences until the building of the new Institute was complete. The gathering in Hitchin recorded by Joshua was attended by about 70 of Isaac Brown's pupils, "some in the front rank of the profession they had followed... All testified to the inspiring character of the teaching and training they had received". William Beck recalled how Isaac Brown had joined John Whiting in forming a Total Abstinence Society, commenting on the moral courage it must have taken to oppose the powerful local Quaker brewing families.

Joseph Lister was at Isaac Brown's Academy as a small boy, with his cousins Samuel and Francis Lucas. A hotel on the site of the school carries his name, but he has been chiefly honoured locally by the naming of Stevenage's hospital, serving much of North Hertfordshire, as the Lister.

## *Mary Chapman*

### 1814 – 1875

There is a refreshing sense of romance and drama around the early story of Mary Whiting, an Ackworth scholar like all her siblings, and the beauty of the family. The first chapter tells of Mary meeting Edward, a young publisher, nephew of Michael Chapman, the Whiting's neighbour in the Market Square. It's a story of young love, secret messages, secret trysts and determination. The friendship was frowned upon by her parents, but her brother Thomas stepped in, and with his support Mary and Edward eloped and were married in Leeds Parish Church. From that point, the setting and activities of Mary's life became very different from anything her siblings were to know. She and Thomas both left the Society. I do not know whether they resigned or were disowned. Until 1859 marriage to a non-Friend in a service taken by a priest made disownment inevitable, and led to a serious loss of young blood in the society. Quaker records have been kept so carefully from the days of George Fox, that it still might well be possible to trace details of Mary's termination of membership. Her brothers and sisters, all of them living comfortably and with broadening horizons, still kept close to the Quaker world of their upbringing and must have felt that Mary had moved into a world quite alien. The Chapmans were soon to be established in Kensington, and Edward's success in his partnership with William Hall soon brought him fame as Dickens' first publisher.

Mary had not only married out but grown away, mixing with men-of-letters, entertaining, travelling abroad (under the wing of Thomas Cook), sending her two daughters, Florence and Meta (Margaret) to an exclusive Academy for Young Ladies. But the Chapman family's compass was not set fair. The one son, Reggie, grew from being a very difficult child to an unmanageable boy. Then it seems as though from being unreliable (and unemployable?) he became actively dishonest to the point of facing criminal charges. The full story is lost, but I believe he eventually married, his wife left him and he disappeared, disgraced, in South Africa. Edward Chapman retired early and travelled widely with his wife. I was told by one of his grand-daughters, who remembered and loved Thomas Whiting as an old man, that those journeys were an attempt to shake off the shadow of Reggie's sad life. Eventually, the Chapmans returned to Hitchin and lived at Elm Lodge in Tilehouse Street. Edward's death was certified by Mary's cousin, Richard Rickman Shillitoe and reported by her brother Thomas. Their two daughters cherished their family history and its Shillitoe links, and made sure that papers and memories were handed on. Meta's son, Frank Gaye, disappeared but not shamefully. He was lost in the early Hollywood and played the name part in a long-forgotten 'Life of Lord Byron.' Never think you can guess the contents of a Quaker family's bran-tub!

## Thomas Cook
### 1808 – 1892

Baptist, committed teetotaller and pioneer in the promotion of safe travel, good food and accommodation for tourists in England and abroad. He often accompanied his passengers and acted as their guide, and enabled many thousands to attend the Crystal Palace Exhibition in 1851. His son, John Cook, who became his partner, organised the dispatch of relief supplies to Paris following the siege of 1870 – 1871.

## F. P. Delmé-Radcliffe
### 1804 – 1875

Described by Bulwer Lytton as a "country gentleman able to hold his own in every field of sport, and no less qualified to take his seat in the cabinet of the statesman or the closet of the philosopher," Frederick Peter Radcliffe of Hitchin Priory came from a long line of squirearchy, many generations being commemorated with plaques and monuments in the great parish church of St Mary's. Radcliffe's world was that of the established county families, soldiers and sportsmen, Anglicans and Tories, co-existing with that of wealthy nonconformist traders and bankers but offering no social mingling. Radcliffe, Etonian, Grenadier, Master of Hounds, gentleman jockey, first-class shot and angler, was also a magistrate and Guardian, and very active in local affairs. He was well-liked, as Hine records, for his "genial, unassuming ways", and may well have been a much more approachable man than some of his Quaker townsmen.

## John Crook
### 1617-1699

A London goldsmith, Justice of the Peace and a member of Cromwell's 1653 Parliament. He became a Quaker after hearing William Dewsbury, 'the apostle of Bedfordshire', preach, and he was imprisoned for his openly expressed beliefs. George Fox stayed with him at his mansion, Beckerings Park, not far from Ampthill, and the huge gatherings held there in 1658 by possibly thousands of Friends from all over the country was the origin of the national yearly Quaker gathering, Yearly Meeting. This was for nearly 300 years based in London but now every fourth year it is the turn of the provinces.

## John Farmer

John Farmer, corn and coal merchant of Market Square, would have lived close to Joshua and Rebecca when they were at Bank House.

## The Fells

Both William and James Fells were described in the 1862 *Post Office Directory* as 'nurseryman, seedsman and florist'. William's address was given as Market Square, but like the Whitings he may also have had ground at Highbury. James was also described as manager of the gas works (gas had come to Hitchin in 1834), grocer and baker. His address was Starling's Bridge, crossing the river Hiz and close to the gas works. Both were sons of Abraham, 'seedsman', of Bucklersbury. In *Hitchin Priory Park* Bridget Howlett describes the part the Fells family played in stocking and enhancing the great Delmé-Radcliffe gardens. I do hope that one day someone with the same skill and knowledge will illuminate the Whiting gardens, a study which might reveal the sturdy survival of a traditional cottage garden in a rapidly developing Victorian suburb. With all the vast differences in their standing and styles, both the Delmé-Radcliffes and Whitings consulted and bought from the Fells. The squire and the clerk both wanted the best for their gardens.

## Myles Birket Foster

### 1825 – 1899

Painter and illustrator from Quaker stock; educated in Hitchin at Isaac Brown's Academy for Young Quakers, where he had his first drawing lessons from Charles Parry. He was very successful, both as a Royal Academy exhibitor and as illustrator. Some of his work sentimentalised the countryside and its people but he studied flowers and trees closely and there is great charm in his prints and watercolours. Bishop's *Handbook to Hitchin* of 1871 is illustrated by Foster, suggesting that he had kept up his links with the town.

# *Gatwards*

In her *People, Places and Past Times of Hitchin* (1974) Aillie Latchmore wrote of the Gatwards as a family of jewellers 'renowned for their business ability'. To Hitchin people today the name Gatward immediately connects with their jewellers' shop in the Market Square; of all our attractive shops, Gatwards probably has the greatest sense of prestige, elegance and history; it dates from 1760 and its premises suggest an even earlier date. The Gatwards were Baptists and musically gifted, supplying organists for 'at least two generations' at Tilehouse Baptist Church. The range of their 'business ability' was remarkable, and it was all concentrated within a few hundred yards. In 1862 (*P.O.D*) Gatward and Jeeves were linen drapers, hosiers and undertakers in the Market Square, as well as watchmakers and jewellers; John Gatward was an ironmonger and agricultural implement maker in the adjoining High Street. In 1869 (*P.O.D*) Mrs Frances Gatward had a fancy repository round the corner in Sun Street. John Gatward's establishment was primarily a foundry, and, in the very centre of the town, roared and belched its way into the twentieth century. In 1893 he bought the Swan Inn next to the present Arcade and hung out a sign for the Swan Iron Works. The one-time Whiting house, where John and Margaret had brought up their family within a stone's throw of a slaughter-house, is shown in a Latchmore photograph of c. 1875 between the Corn Exchange (1853) and a house that had once belonged to Michael Chapman. Long before Burtons, More and Ottakars, the Whiting house had become Hobley's tea-rooms and I can just remember my brother and me being taken to Hitchin by our father to get some idea of one of the family homes.

# *Helen Gilpin*

## 1834 – 1907

Helen Gilpin, sister of Anna Rebecca Whiting, came from a gifted Quaker family which, like the Shillitoes, was entitled to bear arms but had long ago lost any sense of aristocracy. There was a marked ability in the Gilpins for teaching and preaching, and a niece of Helen's, Eva (later Sadler), was a remarkable and adventurous headmistress whose work is now on record in the *ODNB*. Helen had a strong sense of vocation for missionary work and her call was to

Madagascar, where she worked from 1868 – 1895, twice returning to England for a two year furlough. She built up an impressive school for 'girls' (aged from five to forty). In 1870 there were 166 pupils and nine teachers. The school was a Home, and her great delight was contact with the girls. "When we really put our hearts into such work as that… we may not know it, it may not be wise for us to know it, but souls will certainly be won." She shared work on the Malagasy Bible and the taking of Bible classes with Sarah Street.

# *Overend Gurney*

The Overend Gurney affair was a financial collapse of national significance. According to the Barclays Group Archives, for whose help I am very grateful,

> "The new joint-stock banks established from the 1820s onwards were able to raise larger amounts of capital and therefore achieve better stability than the smaller partnerships. However there were still banking crises caused by depressions or 'runs' on reserves. Even after the adoption of limited liability from 1858 onwards, notable failures occurred, and on 'Black Friday' 11 May 1866 Overend, Gurney & Co (the leading London bill brokers and discount house), failed with a staggering debt of £5m just months after being formed into a new limited company in an attempt to save itself from disaster. Shareholders lost £3.5m and some of the Gurney family estates were sold."

Banking historians, Ackrill and Hannah, described Overend Gurney as the largest firm of bill brokers in Europe,

> "particularly aggressive in winning business… treading on the toes of traditional banks… and gradually overstepped themselves. The Gurney families affected were well protected by the banking cousinhood of Barclays, Buxtons and Frys, but there was financial ruin for the many customers who had entrusted money to the firm. It was a scandal as well as a disaster. In 1869 criminal charges were brought against the partners, two of whom were well known Quakers. All were acquitted, but a stain must have spread across the Society of Friends' prized reputation for commercial and personal integrity, and such was the lasting stigma on the Gurney name

that when the firm of Barclay Co. Limited was formed in 1896, with important Gurney partnerships, their name was deliberately omitted from the title.

Shockwaves must surely have gone through the widespread Quaker banking world and would have quickly reached Sharples, Tuke, Lucas and Seebohm in Hitchin, but the entry in Joshua's diary for the day following Black Friday reflects not only his natural sense of composure, but the fact that his work as an employee of the Bank called for the steady care of customers and their accounts, not for any involvement in banking policy. The well-being of his garden and his bees was in his hands; the management of money lay in others."

## *Jackson's*

In the *Post Office Directory* for 1862 George Jackson is listed in the Commercial Section as 'auctioneer, appraiser and estate agent, and agent to the County Fire and Provident Life offices, Bancroft St. and Baldock.'

The business started in the 1800s and closed down in 1989. Its busy and central auction rooms are much missed and the live-stock markets held behind the Cock 'Hotel' are still remembered. As a reminder of how precarious life was in Victorian England with no state pension, no 'income support', no health service, no expectation, – for most people – of any automatic support in care of need or failure, it is worth noting that George Jackson was one of fifteen Insurance Agents listed, representing 23 companies in all, fifteen of them covering Life and Fire. A Quaker, T.G. Pierson, took the agency of 'Indisputable Life' while the Quaker Braunds held 'Atlas', 'Britannia' and 'Clerical, Medical and General Life'.

The *P.O.D* for 1862 has been my main resource not only for Hitchin names and addresses, but giving a clue to the curious distinctions that prevailed between titles. A Hitchin name can move from the Commercial section to that of Private Residents and within that from 'Mr' to 'Esq'. Many rich Quakers accepted the 'esq' though I think the majority of Friends would have percieved the title as 'worldly' however great their standing in the local community. Joshua appears in this edition as 'Private Resident' though he was then living at Bank House with Rebecca, 'over the shop'. His brother Joseph, fellmonger, with his own property in Bancroft was always to be listed as Commercial. At a time when Hitchin's population was around 7000 the *P.O.D.* lists under 500. It would be interesting to know how many 'back-bench' Hitchin friends belonged to the great majority of the unlisted.

## Arthur Latchmore
### 1844-1909

Son of Thomas and Maria and a close friend of Joshua's, Arthur worked in the same bank and died in the same year. He was unmarried and a very keen worker with boys and young men. Together with the Hon. Keith Falconer he founded Hitchin's Blue Cross Temperance Brigade. An obituary notice described him as an invalid "with an extraordinary insight into the needs of those in full health and high spirits".

## Francis Latchmore
### 1839-1899

Frank Latchmore, grocer, was the fifth son of Thomas and Maria, and a cousin of Joshua's. He was educated at Ackworth and a man of wide interests, which as a bachelor he was free to extend and develop. He was a naturalist, a great walker and fisherman, a "pioneer of the pneumatic-tyred bicycle". He joined William Ransom on archaeological digs and was widely respected as a collector of coins and antiquities.

## George Latchmore
### 1838-1904

A son of Thomas and Maria's. He worked alongside his cousin Joshua at the Bank and in 1866 moved to its branch in Luton. While in Hitchin he was a keen supporter of the Mechanics Institute and he was active in adult education all his life. All over the country Quakers were at work in this very wide field, many spurred on by the pioneering achievements of fellow Friend, George Birkbeck. Aillie Latchmore, a descendant of Thomas and Maria, followed the tradition devotedly, and is still remembered in the town for setting up the community she called Hitchin Clubland, which clearly enlivened and enriched the lives of countless young working women and girls.

## Thomas Latchmore

### 1805 – 1875

Quaker, grocer and beekeeper; not to be confused with his son, Thomas Benwell Latchmore, Hitchin's renowned photographer (1832 – 1908). Thomas senior was Joshua's brother-in-law, having married his step-sister, Maria Benwell, only child of Margaret Whiting's first marriage. (This was to Thomas Benwell, a Quaker druggist who died young.) A daughter of the Latchmores was also a Maria, so Joshua uses 'Sister Maria' to avoid confusion. Joshua's sister, Esther, married into another branch of the Latchmore family, so links between the two families were complex and close. Thomas senior had his grocery first in High Street and later in Pound Lane (now Brand Street). His ownership of a field 'opposite the infirmary' is perplexing, because that land would surely have encroached on Butts Close, ten acres of common land with well-used grazing rights. This is one of several topographical puzzles that I have decided to leave unsolved.

This may be the right place to mention my difficulty over the recurring name Benwell. The spelling is clear in the case of Thomas Benwell, druggist (D.Q.B.) and Thomas Benwell Latchmore, Maria's son, but on the Certificate of Marriage for Joshua and Rebecca there are two clearly written signatures for Elizabeth Bennell and Joseph Bennell. The *Oxford Dictionary of Surnames* gives neither name. Though the teasing uncertainty remains, Old Scholars of the Quaker school Sidcot would at once recognise 'Benwell' for one of that named figured largely in the founding of their school.

## Thomas Benwell Latchmore

### 1832 – 1908

Known in the family as T.B., Benwell, Ben, Thomas B., he was the eldest of nine children born in Hitchin to Thomas Latchmore, Quaker grocer, and his wife Maria, née Benwell (1805 – 1866). It is through Maria that the Latchmores have the same direct line to Thomas

Shillitoe that is shared by the Whitings. Her mother Margaret (1784 – 1847) was daughter of Thomas Shillitoe and was first married to Thomas Benwell, a Quaker druggist and apothecary who died only two years later, leaving her with one child, Maria. Margaret married John Whiting, fellmonger, in 1811, and lived for the rest of her life in the Market Square.

Maria grew up with six siblings, went to school at Ackworth and married Thomas Latchmore in 1832. Joshua's diary gives every indication of welcome and natural closeness between Whitings and Latchmores: Maria was his sister, and the Latchmores were part of his family.

After schooldays in Hitchin and at Ackworth, T.B. started work in his father's grocery in the High Street. By 1865 he had branched out with his own interests, establishing a photographic studio in Bancroft (then Bancroft Street). He was to become Hitchin's outstanding recorder, picturing not only buildings of great dignity and charm, but tenements of appalling squalor, and the growth of the new suburbs threatening the much-loved surrounding country-side. His business was continued by his son, and, in spite of the loss of much of the firm's collection, the Latchmores' legacy is one of Hitchin's treasures.

It is interesting that Francis Frith (1822 – 1898), whose famous firm survived until 1971, was also a Quaker and a scholar of Ackworth. In 1860 Frith introduced his photographs of Egypt and Jerusalem with the words "a truthful record is of more value than the most elaborately beautiful picture." T.B. Latchmore's photographs are often sombre, but I am sure that he too was aiming at a truthful record, and his work reflects a grey but convincing picture of mid-Victorian Hitchin.

## Sister Maria

(m. Thomas Latchmore) was Joshua's half-sister, the only child of Margaret Whiting's first marriage to Thomas Benwell, Quaker druggist who died young. It is clear from this diary that there was a strong sense of family bridging all her children. One of her daughters was also Maria, so Joshua may have used 'Sister' to avoid confusion with his niece.

# Francis Lucas

## 1816 – 1896

The youngest son of William Lucas, brewer and diarist and his wife Ann (née Bowly) brother of Samuel Lucas, reluctant brewer and outstanding artist. As a delicate child, he had been given great freedom to be with his father's farm workers and explore fields and woodlands and riversides. Three years of vigorous boarding school life in Bristol developed his many talents and he became a barrister. His marriage to Priscilla Tindall, from which sprang six children, meant so much to him that after her early death he could not speak of her and forbade others to do so. He left the Bar, in which he was very successful, and returned to Tilehouse Street; in 1855 he joined the Bank, then Sharples and Co., as partner. For over 30 years Joshua Whiting and Francis Lucas would have been in daily contact. Both men were much loved in the town and shared a great love of the countryside around it. It is likely that their exchanges would have had more to do with crops, bird-life and the turn of the seasons than the ups and downs of their clients' accounts. In 1889 Lucas published *Sketches of Rural Life*, poems as evocative and down-to-earth as his brother's pen and ink drawings. Some of the characters were identified by Hine: The Ploughman was Jack Pearce, The Carpenter Daniel Joyber, The Miller, Teddy Burr of Charlton. Francis Lucas was a generous man, witty and very good company. His irreverence must have been a tonic to the Society of Friends. Of a Yearly Meeting gathering he wrote "The silence of meeting is such that the drop of $1/_8$th in consols is clearly audible." To quote Hine: "There you have more than wit, you have judgement lightly but irrevocably passed on a generation of friends 'too intent', so Thomas Shillitoe declared, 'on their mortgages and bonds, their interest and compound interest, trying to make a heaven here below'."

# Mad Lucas

## 1813-1874

James Lucas esquire, Lord of the Manor of Redcoat's Green, was Victorian England's most famous hermit and no relation to the Lucas family of Hitchin, Quakers, bankers, brewers and farmers. James's self-imposed isolation of twenty-five years was dramatic, squalid and tragic. After Dickens had turned the spotlight on him in the 1861 Christmas number of *All the Year Round* the G.N.R. advertised excursion trips to Stevenage and visitors came in hundreds to view the wretchedness of his house and maybe have a glimpse of the uncouth man himself.

Richard Whitmore tells of Francis Lucas, banker and the hermit's old friend, being one of his last visitors. On that occasion he had said, "My head has been a good one, but I seem to lose my memory now at times." Messrs. Sharples, Tuke, Lucas and Seebohm had been meticulous in trying to maintain contact with their distressed and demanding client. James Hack Tuke had arranged for James to meet his brother Daniel Hack Tuke, one of the founders of the York Retreat for the Mentally Ill and a renowned specialist. Quaker bankers had certainly proved themselves Friends to poor mad Lucas.

## Samuel Lucas
### 1805 – 1870

Son of William Lucas and brother of Francis. His gift for painting and drawing was apparent from boyhood, but his father took years to acknowledge its importance to him and insisted that his work should be centred on the family brewery and farms. Samuel's gifts were not to be quenched by Quakerly restriction ("if I had been born without hands I must needs have painted with my feet"). He left over 700 watercolours, over 100 oil paintings and volumes of pen and ink drawings. He shared with Francis a great understanding and love of the Hertford-shire landscape both in depth and in detail. All sorts and conditions of Hitchin people appear in his notebooks, touched with comedy and affection. In spite of his local acclaim, his work has never been widely shown. A fine collection is stored in Hitchin Museum and much is still in family hands.

## William Lucas
### 1804 – 1861

This is a chance to recall William Lucas, a leading townsman whose gifted and prolific family had been established in Hitchin for many generations. He was a Quaker, brewer, farmer, naturalist, a man of substance and curiosity who held in balance the demands of his faith, his family, his property, his love for his town and his impatience with its limitations (for his diary – which calls out for a reprint – reflects his enjoyment of wider landscapes and a wider culture).

The years of William Lucas's diary (1829 – 1861) overlap with John Whiting's later years and with Joshua's youth. The latter is mentioned in 1849 as having attended the Peace Congress in Paris, presided over by Victor Hugo. "Our Friend John Whiting's son, Joshua, is gone, and many others in whom a natural desire to see Paris has had more influence than any very strong zeal in the cause."

Both the Whiting and the Lucas families had belonged to the Society of Friends since the 17th century and the first meetings of Quakers in Hitchin had been in the house of an earlier William Lucas. There was a clear difference in their way of life, for the Whitings were incomers to the town and came from a very different Quaker world in which property and land had to be worked for rather than inherited. Besides that, they would always have the strange figure and compelling words of Margaret's father, Thomas Shilltoe, in their minds, warning them of the dangers of property and the seductions of successful trading ("Oh ye middlemen! Ye are filthy men!"). Their strong civic concern would be expressed by their gifts of time and energy rather than by large donations and legacies.

In William Lucas' diary there are four references to John Whiting, all of which I will quote, not only because they give the salty flavour of the writer's style, but because they give such insight both into John Whiting himself, and into some prevailing Quaker scruples and conventions.

"That worthy and honest man, John Whiting, has been labouring with me for unfaithfulness in regard to Months, and among other things stated that it operated against my being made useful in our Society. Alas, that such narrow grounds of fellowship should exist!"

(17/3/1839)

"John Whiting, who is the great advocate and support of teetotalism in Hitchin, has been frequently obliged by doctor's orders to resume Beer and today we hear he is again ill. Total abstinence is certainly irrational, unchristian and inexpedient, temperance is quite another thing."

(11/4/1841)

Writing of the Town Mission Society, "Uncle Allen (Stafford Allen), John Whiting and Joshua Ransom taking a kind of Ultra Friend view, could not feel easy to join this......We ought to seek rather grounds of agreement than points of difference."

(7/9/1845)

"Today our friend J.W. had to appear before the Bench of Magistrates to answer an information under the Health of Towns Act for establishing a new Fellmonger yard down Bancroft. After a long hearing he was acquitted. His integrity and truthfulness did more for him than any legal ability could have done."

(6/8/1850)

## Joseph Morris

Kelly's *Bedfordshire Directory* for 1869 gives Mr Joseph Morris and Mr John Morris as private residents in Ampthill. John Morris is also given as 'brewer' in the commercial section with Frederick Morris, grocer and ironmonger. The predominantly Quaker Morris family is said by the county's historian Joyce Godber to have has a greater influence on Ampthill than any other single family. Through the eighteenth century they were blacksmiths and grocers, able to build up considerable property and funds until another earlier John became a brewer, employing architects to build the impressive Avenue House, "a model of Georgian taste at its best", but of an elegance and grandeur exceeding that of any Hitchin Quaker's house in Bancroft, and provoking Elders' disapproval. John became an Anglican and is on record as having insisted that his employees in the brewery should attend the parish church and none other, while Lord Holland, a neighbouring aristocrat, said that all who worked on *his* estate could follow any religious practice they chose. By 1851, the Sunday attendance at Ampthill Meeting House (with seating for over 200) had dwindled to close on twenty.

## John Ransom and Benslow

The name of John Ransom and his son and daughter Alfred and Jane all appear on the Whitings' Certificate of Marriage, and they reappear constantly in the diary. John's house, close both to the railway station and the town centre, and healthfully above the stench and sewage of the latter, is still standing, and was first known as Benslow Hill House. There are still some fine specimen trees in the gardens, and a sense of style shared by another Ransom house just across the lane, Fairfield, built by William Ransom on what had been bare hill-top land. Benslow House had some years of renown, for two years after John's death in 1867 the Ladies College, later to be established in Cambridge as Girton, was set up, mocked at by some and marvelled at by others. It had considerable support from local Friends, and two of the first six students were Quakers. Joshua made no mention of it and would probably have greatly missed the Ransom connection. Later the house became, and still is, a nursing home. Fairfield was bought by the Seebohms, and thanks to the generosity of Esther, a daughter of Frederic's, the Rural Music School Association had its base there and the house renamed as Little Benslow Hills. The Rural Music School Association was reborn as the Benslow Music Trust and the greatly extended buildings are now home to a nationally known music centre for amateur players and a great cultural and social asset for the town.

# William Ransom

## 1826 – 1914

The scope of William Ransom's gifts and activities is vividly outlined by Reginald Hine: "you will not know whether to class him as pharmacist, botanist, archaeologist, naturalist, publicist, magistrate, benefactor or Quaker". He came from sturdy East Anglian Quaker stock, long established in Hitchin, where his father, John, was both farmer and miller. William attended Isaac Brown's Academy in Hitchin, where other Quaker boys included Joseph Lister, Birket Foster and a lifetime friend, Joseph Pollard, botanist and naturalist of Highdown. William served an apprenticeship with the Quaker pharmaceutical firm of Southall's in Birmingham. He qualified in pharmacy and by 1846 was able to start his own business in Hitchin. All manner of medicinal herbs were extracted at Ransom's: flowers, roots, bark, were all either brought in from the villages around or cultivated on Ransom land. Lavender was an especial crop, and Hitchin lavender had great renown in Victorian days, remembered today in the museum by special Lavender days, by the preservation of Perks and Llewellyn's old chemist's shop and perfumery, and above all by the recent revival of lavender growing at Cadwell Farm near Hitchin.

However enlightened the Quaker firm of Southall may have been, the years in Birmingham would have given William a stark picture of the living conditions of the city's workforce, and the diary of his first years back in Hitchin show him to have been not only intensely interested in the coming of the railway ("opening up," to quote Hine again, "not only a new world and a new range of possibilities, but exposing, by navvies' spades, great geological and archaeological riches") and amazing technological advances made visible to the public in the 1851 Great Exhibition of the Industry of Nations, but acutely aware of the country's need for political or social reform. In 1858 William married the eldest Southall daughter, Anna Mary, and their one son Francis, another very gifted man, took over the business, greatly expanding and developing it, leaving his father with many years in which to devote his energy to the community. He served in such roles as magistrate, County Councillor, Governor of the Grammar School, Governor of the Hospital, Vice President of the Mechanics Library and Reading Room, and was a generous benefactor to the town. His service to the Society of Friends was constant, at both local and national levels, with special concern for temperance and adult education. With James Tuke, he was a founder member of the Friends Foreign Mission Association which was to be based for many years in Hitchin, where the house Lavendercroft was a haven for missionaries' families (and later for war time refugees).

The very full obituary in the weekly *Friend* ends on a note of Quaker restraint and orthodoxy: "Thus has passed this useful life… a life spent in the service of God and humanity." There may be still more to know about this remarkable man. Meanwhile, thanks to the William Ransom Physic Garden flourishing next door to the Museum and Library, many of us have a daily reminder of his life-long love and study of herbs. Those who know Little Benslow Hills, formerly the Ransom home, Fairfield, have the great trees of his arboretum to enjoy for many years to come. They have a special place in Hitchin's landscape.

A company brochure of 1998, introducing William Ransom & Son plc, stated "Ransom has been at the forefront of natural extract technology since 1846." For all these years Ransom's has had an outstanding reputation in Hitchin, and till last year was based in Bancroft, at the heart of the old town. For Quakers, it is in many ways the last link with the days when Hitchin was known as 'the Quaker town'. Though Lucases, Seebohms, Tukes and many other established Quaker families have moved away, it is good to remember that presiding over Hitchin's Forum, a society devoted to the care and well-being of the town, is a member of the Ransom family.

## *Benjamin Seebohm*
### (1798 – 1871)

Benjamin, father of Frederic, was born into a German Quaker family. He settled in England and prospered in the Bradford wool industry. Before marrying Esther Wheeler of Hitchin, he had travelled widely in England, Ireland and North America, being 'liberated for service in the ministry' by his Monthly Meeting, Brighouse. There was great power in his spoken words, but as well as being known as 'the Golden Trumpet of the North', he was respected for strange telepathic insights, and, like Thomas Shillitoe, was acutely sensitive to the inner dilemmas of friends and strangers. He moved to Luton in 1861. Ten years later he died in London in the course of Yearly Meeting, managing to send his friends "a final message of his earnest desire that the Society might be preserved on its sure foundation, Jesus Christ, the same yesterday, today and forever."

In his last letter he had written of his certainty of redemption and afterlife ("like Paul who did not say we hope or believe but we know"). Joshua was not present at the meeting for burial. He would have been among old friends and family at the heart of this impressive occasion, but stayed at the Bank, "as D. Lloyd wanted to go."

## *Frederic Seebohm*
### 1833 – 1912

Historian and banker. His early life in Yorkshire was spent "in a home of simplicity, integrity, intellectual stimulus and deep spirituality." He was called to the Bar, but in 1857 entered the Bank of Sharples and Exton and married Mary Ann, a daughter of William Exton, who was to inherit not only the rambling Hermitage and its seven acre garden behind Bancroft, but its contents and a large fortune. Frederic remained a partner of the Bank for many years but, throughout his life, history had been his main study, and his scholarly and innovative works brought him not only honourary degrees but wide renown. He was active in local and national affairs and a generous supporter of many Hitchin enterprises, most particularly the Boys' and Girls' Grammar Schools.

Victoria Glendinning's *A Suppressed Cry* is required reading for its evocation of the Hitchin Seebohms and of Hitchin itself, with the fraying but still golden thread of the world of Quaker bankers running throughout. Strangely, it is the sombre story of her great-aunt Winnie's short life that brings the painful message of vitality into that world, for her longings and frustrations are a very human cry which, tragically, was never heard or understood.

Reginald Hine's account of Frederic in *Hitchin Worthies* tells of his many friendships, but scarcely touches on his family life. It is an impressive but rather daunting picture of great achievement and unblemished rectitude, but some of Frederic Seebohm's words shine out: "we may have to learn to live without a cut and dried theology" and "the goal of civilisation, the art of living in civilised society". His "history is wrapt up in the biography of great men" calls for debate, and it is all the more interesting that Victoria Glendinning, his descendant, should have quoted George Eliot – words that I have often thought of in connection with Joshua and Rebecca Whiting: "For the growing good of the world is partly dependant on unhistoric acts; and that things are not as ill with you and me as they might have been, is half owing to the number who lived faithfully a hidden life, and rest in unvisited tombs."

# Joseph Stickney Sewell

## 1819 – 1900

Linked to Ackworth both as scholar and outstanding master, his lifelong commitment was to education and communication. He came to Hitchin as a widower in the 1860's and joined the Sharples, Tuke, Lucas and Seebohm Bank. His interest in foreign mission work focussed on Madagascar and in 1867 he left for the island (a three month voyage), staying until 1876, doing remarkable work as teacher and preacher. He was greatly supported by James Hack Tuke and the founding of the Friends Foreign Mission Association in 1868 owed much to these two friends. William Tallack, writing on Hitchin Friends in the *Friends Quarterly Examiner* for 1907, made the interesting comment that "the most important speciality of the Hitchin Friends has been their zeal for, and great service to, the cause of foreign missions… Its several secretaries, Watson Grace, Charles Linney and Dr William Wilson, have found Hitchin a most appropriate place of residence and of stimulus to action. The Ransom family and other local friends cordially co-operated with them in the good work." On his return to England he became Editor of *The Friend*, serving for thirteen years.

## Lucy Sewell

### 1845-1895

Lucy Sewell had before her a life of devoted service in Madagascar which was to end tragically. She left England in 1872 to marry William Johnson (1842-1895). He was an old Scholar of Ackworth, a teacher and a fellow missionary of her father's, both seeing their work as "a mission of love." William and Lucy worked together in Madagascar for over twenty years, taking two spells of furlough. They were beloved there and it was their home. In 1895, in a wild uprising, they and their child, Blossom, were brutally murdered. At his farewell meeting in Hitchin in 1867 Joseph had read from Corinthians: "Finally, brethren, farewell. Be perfect. Be of good comfort, be of one mind, live in peace; and the God of love and peace shall be with you."

## Isaac Sharp the elder

### 1806 – 1897

Based in Middlesbrough, he had a long and close association with Ayton. For many years he was secretary to Joseph Pease MP remembered as the first Quaker to sit in Parliament and for having established the right of members to affirm rather than take the oath. Isaac Sharp travelled widely as missionary and minister, "a ready fund of anecdote and abundant humour endearing him to the inmates of lonely mission stations and isolated dwellings from the northern to the southern polar circle."

## Isaac Sharp the younger
### 1847 – 1917

The two Isaac Sharps were both prominent Friends, not obviously related and over a period of years, easy to confuse. The younger Isaac was educated at Bootham and at University College, London (the undenominational University of London was founded in 1836). Years as a teacher culminated in his headship of the Woodlands School in Hitchin, which opened in 1873, taking over the house and grounds in Bancroft that had once belonged to Joseph Sharples. From 1890 to the year of his death he was Recording Clerk to London (now 'Britain') Yearly Meeting, a job demanding great knowledge and authority. The title is unchanged, but today's holder of the office would be thought of as the principal administrator. Isaac Sharp was an outstanding historian and served as the Society's librarian at Devonshire House until that office was formally established. *The Friend's* obituary brought the drab title of Recording Clerk to life, recalling his "rich cheery voice," his "kindness and charm" and "deep sense of humour". In the large gathering that was to meet in 1909 for Joshua's burial service Isaac Sharp spoke memorably of his gentleness, kindness and Christian grace… a man full of love for justice, full of mercy, unselfishness, calmness and serenity of mind… The end of that man is peace."

## Joseph Sharples
### 1791 – 1871

The Sharples name and male line died with Joseph Sharples. In spite of his standing in Hitchin as Quaker banker and philanthropist he is a shadowy figure in Hitchin records and in those of the Library at Friends House, but thanks to an unknown obituarist and a cutting in the Lawson Thompson† Scrapbooks in Hitchin Museum, he can be brought to life, filling out the many sketches by Samuel Lucas. He was an only child, lame and very sickly, but, to the pride of his nurse, not only grew to manhood and marriage, but became "a very expert and elegant skater". "Not particularly disposed to literature or

science, he took a lively interest in ingenious inventions, improvements in carriages, new contrivances for the convenience of travellers, expediencies for meeting the little emergencies of the road". He enjoyed "his garden, his grotto, canal and conservatories, and his horses... His table was plain and bountiful. In his establishment quiet, order and punctuality everywhere prevailed.....
He was seldom away from home; could be found at any time and on any occasion when the interests of the town or neighbourhood were concerned was always ready... He did much good and was known to have done even more privately".

Joseph Sharples was born and died in a fine Bancroft house (no. 21, The Woodlands), across the road from Ransoms and Seebohms and close to the Tukes at the Croft. He was in early partnership with William Exton and John Bassett and became a very successful banker. In 1828 he married Elizabeth Ransom, a sister of William. Their one child, Eliza (involved in the Ragged School funded by her father) married Alexander Peckover, later Lord Peckover of Wisbech, and died in 1862, leaving three young daughters. Joseph's beloved wife died a few years later, after which "he drooped visibly". Joshua's diary entry in 1871, "Joseph Sharples died this year – everything sold by auction at the house" gives a bleak picture of the end of a family line.

## Ann Shillitoe

Ann Shillitoe lived in Tottenham, where the family connections were strong. Thomas Shillitoe had only one brother, William, and it seems probable that Ann was his unmarried daughter, Margaret Whiting's aunt and great-aunt to Joshua (though more comfortably referred to as 'aunt').

## Richard Rickman Shillitoe

### 1818 – 1885

A cousin of Joshua's, grandson of Thomas, and a respected Hitchin doctor. The Shillitoe name in Hitchin is now probably better known by its record of activity in medicine and the law and in the Parish of St. Mary's than it is through the remarkable story of Thomas, the fervent Quaker.

# *Thomas Shillitoe*
## 1754-1836

Quaker minister and missionary and traveller extraordinary. Thomas was born an Anglican and lived to become one of the nineteenth century's great Quaker messengers and a friend of Stephen Grellet, Elizabeth Fry and Peter Bedford. Hitchin was his home for ten years (he was born and died in Tottenham) and here he wrote his journal, *The Life, Labours and Travels of Thomas Shillitoe in the Service of the Gospel of Jesus Christ*. It is clear from the journal and from the family memories that persist that there was no particular social cause to which he attached himself. His mission was to bring salvation to the destitute, a message of hope and encouragement to the imprisoned, the impoverished, the drunk, the dissolute. Though he was a man of crippling nervousness, he had a lion's courage when it came to visiting the powerful – he besought George IV to live a better life, crossed Europe to have audience with Czar Alexander I and crossed the Atlantic to plead with slave owners in North Carolina. He sat with the families of executed handloom weavers in Yorkshire and was to be found praying in prisons and gin-shops. William Tallack, a Victorian Quaker, described Thomas as being a man of much humour, "good without being disagreeable", with "cheerful spirits, even exuberant". To Friends he made a special call to simplicity. He understood how the Quaker flair for success in commerce was putting fetters on the original impetus to a return to primitive Christianity. He prayed that his children and grandchildren would not become traders and dealers, "middlemen", "those double-minded folk!" When he took long journeys on foot in England he would wear labourer's clothes so that he could pay for his board by farmwork, but it should be remembered that on many of his travels abroad he would have been the guest of Quaker "middlemen" whose hospitable trading stations were spread around the world.

## *Steeds*

The Steeds were Quaker brewers in Baldock, "All planted by her own hands" emphasises that many, like Rebecca, was a hands-on, spade-in gardener, exercising choice and carrying out the job. They may well have enjoyed the freedom of out-door physical exercise as much the gratifying results of gardening.

# Louis and Sarah Street

Louis (1833-1892) and his wife Sarah were from Ohio. They were the first American Quaker missionaries to work out of their country. They accompanied Joseph Sewell but had to return in 1872 because of illness. Louis helped revise the *Malagasy Bible*, started a Malagasy newspaper and working on a Malagasy/English dictionary. An undated cutting from the Lawson Thompson albums describes a Flower Show held by the Hitchin Adult Sunday Schools at the Workman's Hall. Among many traditional, routine, lovingly prepared exhibits (fruit, flowers, vegetables, needlework, straw plaiting, and bread) the following entry appears: "Miss Sewell and Mrs. W Ransom sent a collection of curiosities from Madagascar, among them some long plaits of hair cut from the heads of some of Mrs Street's scholars, who had no other gifts to send their kind friends in Hitchin."

# Lawson Thompson

## 1837-1919

Lawson Thompson was a Quaker tradesman with unusual accomplishments and flair. His father, John, ('tailor, woollendraper and clothier' – *P.O.D* 1862) married Mary Lucas and there was a rich talent in their offspring. Lawson was well known in Hitchin for his lively good humour, his practical concern for the town (particularly for its poor), his collection of books and prints and his surprising thespian gifts. To Reginald Hine, a friend of his last years, Elmside, the handsome house shared by Lawson and two of his sisters, was "the gathering place of wit and hospitality and human kindness." It is now a much-valued residential home under the wing of the Methodist Church. Hine makes no mention of the trade that the Thompsons followed so successfully, describing Lawson as having "the air of a gentleman of leisure." A man of great good humour and style, he was much in demand at local theatricals, comic turns being his speciality. His relationship with Hitchin Meeting must surely have been strained, and Hine reports that Lawson was 'disciplined' by Friends for exhibiting himself in a French play ('Ici on parle français') at the Town Hall, but he stayed within the Society. Hine quotes a passage from the puritan Richard Baxter that Lawson had doubly underlined: "Whilst we wrangle here in the dark, we are dying and passing to the world that will decide all controversies; the safest passage thither is peaceable holiness."

Whatever happened to the Lawson Thompson collection of books and prints, Hitchin Museum has in its Students' room the bound volumes of Scrapbooks, started by John Thompson as 'The Hitchin Book' and continued by his son. These massive books are a treasured local resource, hundreds of pages of 19th century ephemera, and perhaps above all a reminder of the scope and quality of the old local newspapers, rich in detailed stories, obituaries, anniversaries, advertisements, happenings abroad, in London, in the villages. With the scrapbooks, with the continuing hospitality of Elmside and the memory of a lively maverick Quaker, Hitchin has good reason to offer warm thanks to Lawson Thompson.

## Uncle Thomas

Joshua's mother, Margaret, daughter of Thomas and Mary Shillitoe, had a sister Hannah who married Thomas Dawson, almost certainly 'Uncle Thomas'. The Tottenham connections were strong, and would have included Hannah's family and 'Aunt Ann Shillitoe' who appears later in the diary. *See photo page xiv.*

## Anna M Whiting (later Harvey)

### 1851-1934

Annie, as she was always known, was the eldest of the family of John and Anna Rebecca Whiting of Leeds, the city in which she spent nearly all her life. She and her sister Mary and her brothers John Edmund and William were regular visitors to the Hitchin uncles, aunts and cousins. After schooldays at the Mount, York, she joined Robert and Christine Alsop in their relief work in Paris following the Franco-Prussian War and in 1873 she married William Harvey of Leeds, a Quaker in the silk trade, who retired early to follow a life of quiet philanthropy and practical service both in Leeds and in the affairs of the Society of Friends. He had studied at University College, London, and was a man of very wide culture. In *The Friend's* obituary Annie's intellectual ability was commented on, her "knowledge of and interest in politics, reform and the history and literature of Europe and her own country led our thoughts to a wider world of delight and contemplation." Quite apart from that and from the impressive record of her faithful good works in Leeds, I think it was her special sweetness and sense of fun that her many grandchildren (of whom I am one) will have remembered best. *See photo page xiv.*

## *Cousin William*

Joshua's father, John Whiting, was one of twelve children. His brother Richard married Elizabeth Harvey and their only son, William (1806 – 1889) lived in Tottenham. He was a constant visitor to his Hitchin cousins.

# *Notes*

1 **Quaker calendar:** 16th October, 16.10, 16X, or 16th Tenth Month? Wednesday, Fourth Day, or 4th Day? The questions arise because Early Friends objected to using the names of the days and months that derived from the names of gods and goddesses. September to December were acceptable as their origins were numerical, but the pattern was set and all days, all months were numbered, with Sunday as First Day, as it remains in many American meetings and is still to be found in England, though not on official documents.

In Joshua's lifetime, many Friends were realising that some of their cherished usages should be put aside and seen as part of their Society's developing history but not as bedrock; there was a greater readiness to conform to the idiom of the business and political world. There were wide variations in the manner of dating, and for the sake of simplicity, dear to Quakers, I have decided to follow modern usage in the transcription of his diary.

Joshua's diary contains references to 'Xmas', 'St Swithun's', 'Good Friday', 'Michaelmas', all pointing to his easy acceptance of common usage.

2 **Highbury:** Until the 1860s Highbury would have been an undisturbed area of farmland, orchards and gardens. With views across the town to the Chilterns beyond, and being only a short walk to the Railway Station opened in 1850, it was soon to become a favoured suburb. It is difficult today to picture the landscape bare of the arboretum planted by William Ransom at Fairfield (Little Benslow Hills), by those responsible for Hitchin Cemetery (1850's) and others who planted for the future. "The family garden" referred to by Joshua would have once belonged to John

Whiting and may have included land once belonging to his father-in-law, Thomas Shillitoe, who had lived for some years at the top of Hollow Lane.

3 **Fishponds:** The diary refers to 'the Fishpond Garden', 'Fish Pond Garden', 'Fish Ponds', 'Fish Pond closes'. The large stretch of land, with many small ponds, abutting the Sharples estate on the north side of Bancroft, included two fields known as Little Fish Pond Close and Great Fish Pond Close. 'Close' could mean an enclosure, an enclosed field or a farmyard and these definitions may have become blurred. In 1894, at the Sun Hotel, the auctioneer, George Jackson, handled the sale of 'Building land for the erection of Villa Residences, from a portion of the beautifully timbered land called Fishpond Closes, with a frontage to Fishpond Road." Some of these 'Villa Residences' remain. The adjoining 'beautiful timbered land' and the fine gardens of the Sharples estate were five years later to give a very attractive setting to the buildings of the Grammar School (now Hitchin Boys School). Local charities and private philanthropy (the Quaker families of Lucas, Seebohm, Sharples and Ransom were outstandingly generous) ensured that the two Grammar Schools, for boys and girls, had buildings of outstanding dignity and grounds of great beauty.

4 **The Bank:** Although the bank referred to in the diary was often known in the mid-19th century as the Hertford-shire Hitchin Bank, its origins were in Bedfordshire, in a grocer's shop in Leighton Buzzard, in which banking had developed and flourished as a sideline. In 1820 three partners started an independent bank in Hitchin. Two, both Quakers, Joseph Sharples and William Exton moved there and were the fore-runners of Hitchin's influential banking families. When Joshua and Rebecca started their married life at Bank House, the business was known as Sharples, Tuke, Lucas and Seebohm. The scene was set until the formation of Barclays in 1896 and the imposing façade remains.

The Bedfordshire connection remained strong, for the original bank opened branches in Ampthill and Luton. Reinforcing this was the Quaker link, often a blood tie, as from 1800 to 1865, when many meetings were regrouped, Hitchin and Ampthill were in the same Monthly Meeting, and it's clear that Joshua remained loyal to his Bedfordshire friends.

In 1861 the Whitings returned from their wedding-tour (a phrase I think they would have preferred to 'honeymoon') to live in what had been Joshua's bachelor quarters at Bank House. Here they would have had the care of the young men who had 'gained a seat', 'obtained a clerkship' or 'been given a desk' in this well-established firm. Their brothers might have followed apprenticeships with grocers, drapers, shoemakers, chemists, all manner of trades and careers that were open to dissenters. They would expect to live "over the shop" or at least under the watchful eye of their employer and his wife, and in Bank House the Whitings would have been in loco parentis to several Warners, a Marsh, a Sheppard, a Latchmore and, memorably a Clarke, who stands out as the only person mentioned in the diary as seriously unpleasant. One longs to know why his time in Hitchin was cut short, and what he'd done to offend his kind guardians so deeply.

5   **Bees:** *What well appointed commonwealths! where each*
*Adds to the stock of happiness for all;*
*Wisdom's own forums! whose professors teach*
*Eloquent lessons in their vaulted hall!*
*Galleries of art! and schools of industry!*
*Stories of rich fragrance! orchestra of song!*
*What marvellous seats of hidden alchymy!*
*How oft, when wandering far and erring long,*
*Man might learn truth and virtue from the BEE!*

*Sir John Bowring (1792-1872)*

6   **The Folly:** There are so many references to 'our Folly hives' that I was determined to find out just where they would have been. Hitchin still has a long footpath, Folly Path, leading from Stevenage Road towards the Cemetery and a map of 1834 shows Folly Cottages on the other side of the road. Folly Path cuts across the stretch of land called Sunnyside, which was named after the Ragged School built in 1830, for children from the Folly. Jeeves, noted Hitchin builders over the period of the town's Victorian expansion, had extensive brick kilns, gravel pits and chalk pits at the Folly. The Ordnance Survey map of 1851 shows Hitchin Folly as an area, and a short distance towards Stevenage gives Hitchin

Old Folly, a wooded expanse, with a house-sized property. Nowhere have I found any reference to a building that we would recognise as a Folly, no record of any eccentric or grandiose structure. Remembering that the Folly area lies around the top of Hitchin Hill, I believe the answer may lie in the O.E.D. where, using a quotation from Richard Jefferies, the word, as dialect, is defined as 'a clump of fir trees on the crest of a hill'.

7   The old proverb "**March dust** is worth a king's ransom"appeared in *The Times* 'Weather eye' column for March 7th 2006 as:
>   *A bushel of March dust is a thing worth the ransom of a king.*
An 18th century version was:
>   *A peck of March dust and a shower in May,*
>   *Makes the corn green and the gardens gay.*

Joshua would probably have built up his stock of gardening and farming lore from ready talk with countrymen and gardeners rather than from the printed word, but references make it clear that he had Gilbert White's *Selborne* at hand.

8   **Gardens:** *'What greater pleasure can there be than to smell the sweet odour of herbes, trees, and fruites, and to behold the goodly colour of the same… yea nothing more discovereth unto us the great and incomprehensible worke of God, that of one little Pepinsede, Nut or small plant, may come forth infinite of the same fruit, which also doth shine and shew forth itselfe unto us especially in the Spring time, by their diversity of shootes, blossoms and buds and in divers Kindes of nature, by the goodnesse and mightie power of the great Lorde and Creator towards his people.'*

>   Leonard Mascall *A Book of the Arte and Maner how to plant and grafte*, 1572 quoted by Hilda M. Coley, *Our Heritage of Fruits* 1937.

9   **The value of the £:** Costs and prices are constantly noted in the diary. From the nature of his upbringing and his occupation (and very possibly from his own temperament) Joshua would have been a careful spender. A key to the scale of The Whiting's expenses is given by the fact that in 1865 the pound had the value of £45 in today's money. *See opposite a bill of Joshua's.*

10  **Monthly Meeting:** Although at the time of writing a much-discussed reorganisation is on its way, the Religious Society of Friends, in its basic structure, has changed very little over 300 years. George Fox, our Christian founder, realised the paramount need for a firm framework for the group he had attracted; his followers were alight with enthusiasm, highly charged with individuality

and the urge to experiment. This extraordinarily magnetic man was both prophet and administrator, and held our awkward ancestors together. He dealt with space by a network of areas, and with time by arranging area meetings at weekly, monthly, quarterly and yearly intervals. The weekly meetings, preparative and 'recognised' are the local focus of worship and attendance, usually weekly though the recognised meetings may meet less frequently. The monthly meeting holds its members with scrupulous recording and carries out the business of the group. I hope it may be interesting and helpful to include here two references from *Whitaker's Almanack*, one from its first publication in 1868 and the second from the current edition for 2006.

## Religious Society of Friends

After paragraphs on the Established Church and on Methodists, Congregationalist and Baptists *Whitaker's* gave a long list of 'minor religious sects' which included Roman Catholics, Jews, Latter Day Saints, Recreative Religionists, Peculiar People, Glassites and Sandemanians. Unitarians were chief of this group and the Society of Friends in second place, consisting of "about 17,000 members ... and 265 recorded ministers... their places of worship in England and Wales are 365."

The entry for the 2006 *Almanack* (from the long detailed chapter headed 'Religion in the UK') makes an interesting contrast, and I am grateful to the publishers for their permission to reprint in full:

> ### Religious Society of Friends (Quakers)
> *Quakerism is a movement, not a church, which was founded in the 17th century by George Fox and others in an attempt to revive what they saw as 'primitive Christianity". The movement was based originally in the Midlands, Yorkshire and north-west England, but there are now Quakers in 36 countries around the world. The colony of Pennsylvania, founded by William Penn, was originally Quaker.*
> *Emphasis is placed on the experience of God in daily life rather than on sacraments or religious occasions. There is no church calendar. Worship is largely silent and there are no appointed ministers; the responsibility for conducting a meeting is shared equally among those present. Social reform and religious tolerance have always been important to Quakers, together with a commitment to non-violence in resolving disputes.*
> *There are 338,000 Quakers world-wide, with over 15,500 in Great Britain and Ireland. There are about 500 meetings in Great Britain.*
> *Central Offices: (Great Britain) Friends House, 173-177 Euston Road, London NW1 2BJ. T 020-7663-1000 F 020-7663 1001 W www.quaker.org.uk*
> © *Whitaker's Almanack 138th edition A & C Black (Publishers) Ltd. 2005*

11  **Ampthill** was, until 1865, part of Hitchin Monthly Meeting. From 1866 it was grouped with Luton and Leighton Monthly Meeting but it is clear from the Diary that the Whitings' connections with the area and their many Ampthill friendships continued as strongly as before (and may well have been easier to maintain with the arrival of the railway in Ampthill in 1867). Ampthill Meeting closed in 1880. The Meeting House was sold, though it still stands and is now in use as a bakery. Bedford Friends revived the Meeting in 1989 and a group of Friends now meets every

month, using a room in the Baptist Chapel. The banking and brewing themes run through the histories of Ampthill and Hitchin Quakers and it would be interesting to compare and contrast the part played by Friends in the story of the two towns.

12 **Pic nics** originated in France in the 18th Century and were rather grand entertainments. In Victorian England they became open-air parties to which everyone contributed and they are still a mainstay of English family life, an opportunity for generations to mix up and to enjoy the accompanying dilemmas and comedies. Since Victorian days picnics have been one of the few social occasions at which Quakers excel, and even now may resemble a strange tribal gathering.

13 **Travel:** The record of trips and journeys taken by Joshua and Rebecca is not only interesting in itself but gives clues to the great variety of ways in which they were able to travel. First of all, by today's standards, Joshua was a great walker, covering considerable distances without comment on mileage or practical difficulties. Walking was customary, a part of life, and in breaking that ancient human tradition, we have lost untold opportunities for observation, reflection and encounter. However, the Whitings, in a modest way, and with the means, were ready for adventure and took readily to rail travel, though there was an abundance of horse-drawn vehicles at hand for local visits which Rebecca could not manage on foot. Joshua was frequently 'driving' and 'riding' to places, with mention of 'fly', bus', 'wagonette', 'phaeton', 'trap'. Horse-drawn transport was hugely diverse and the style in which it was maintained was an instant indicator of social class. By chance I recently came upon *An Assemblage of 19th Century Horses and Carriages* from the sketches of William Francis Freelove (1846-1920). Freelove was a Quaker, a solicitor's clerk, living in Surrey. Like Joshua Whiting, he probably never owned a carriage of his own, probably never owned a horse. He was fascinated by all that was horse-drawn, from State Coach to Carrier's Cart. The seventy-one drawings date from 1871-1873, detailed, vivid, comic, rich in pictures of drivers, passengers and street scenes. Joshua and Rebecca would have travelled locally either in a friend's 'Pleasure Vehicle' (maybe, sometimes hiring one?) or a 'Public Vehicle', bus, van or cab. I am very grateful to Jennifer Lang for having

compiled such an enriching book to enliven our idea of what trundled, rolled and clattered along Victorian roads and byways.

14 By **'liberate'** probably all Joshua meant was that he and Rebecca would, by a period of house-sitting, enable the Hagens (who were in some ways related) to go off on their August holiday with easy minds. There is also a special Quaker sense to the word, which links it with the Society's use of 'concern'. If Friends have an over-powering sense of guidance, and feel under an imperative to proclaim a message or act in a certain way, they are said to be 'under concern', and will bring the matter to their Meeting, who will hear the concern, testing its validity in thoughtful prayer and worship as well as discussion. The Friend would hope to be 'liberated', given the Meeting's concurrence and blessing (and possibly funds to support the concern). The Meeting would give the Friend a Quakerly letter of introduction known as a Travelling Minute, for use on journeys among Meetings where the concern would be voiced.

15 **Orchard:** From Latin 'hortus' and Old English 'ortyeard' a garden, "an enclosed piece of ground for the purposes of horticulture; a garden for herbs and fruit trees," (*O.E.D.*). It would seem that by the mid-nineteenth century gardens and orchards were being regarded as quite separate areas for the 'Florists Journal' in 1845 stated that "orchards are portions of ground appropriated to the growth of fruit trees only." In the Whiting's small domain everything seemed to grow so comfortably together that maybe their gardens were closer to the old sense of 'orchard', with no strict plan of plots and borders. Their gardens were clearly bee-friendly, as would have been customary at the time, and the hands-on upkeep of a garden would have been a natural part of middle class family life. Joshua's interest and knowledge would certainly have been enriched by his Ackworth schooldays, for boys were given their own strips in the Great Garden, and school records tell of the enthusiasm with which they were tended and the expert knowledge the boys could draw on. In Hitchin there would be ongoing exchange of plants and gardening lore among such expert friends as Alfred Ransom and Arthur Latchmore.

16 **Park River:** This would be Hitchin's still very elusive and vulnerable little river, the Hiz. It rises at Wellhead above the

hamlet of Charlton and runs through Priory Park and the centre of the old town. It has its glory moment passing St Mary's where Hitchin can boast its own Backs, and there are several short stretches where it is cherished and watched for our own enjoyment. The Purwell and the Oughton are Hitchin's even smaller rivers that join the Hiz and together 'reach the Ivel outside Biggleswade.

17  **Line of beauty:** On a bowl made during the Siege of Mafeking the following lines were inscribed a few days after the town's relief:

> *Straight is the line of duty,*
> *Curved is the line of beauty.*
> *Follow the straight line:*
> *Thou shalt see*
> *The curved will ever follow thee.*

Round the bowl the straight and curved lines cross and intertwine. 'The line of beauty' according to the *O.E.D.* is "the curve (resembling a slender elongated S) held by Hogarth to be a necessary element in all beauty of form". In garden design it suggests not only the influence of the Picturesque, but an amplitude of space, in which the practicality of straight paths (nearest being straightest) can give way to the pleasure for the eye in winding paths and the pleasure in wondering what lies round the bend. There are still some distinct 'lines of beauty' in the old Ransom garden and arboretum in what was formerly Fairfield and is now Little Benslow Hills. These date from the mid-nineteenth century and, newly planted, would have been well-known to Joshua. The Whiting garden and orchards were obviously on a quite different scale, but it is interesting that Joshua was evidently so taken by the idea of the 'line of beauty' that with Jim Brown's help he made his own for the garden of Spring Cottage.

18  See John Ransom (biographical sketches) for **Benslow.**

19  **Union:** Following the Poor Law of 1834, local Boards of Guardians were appointed, and overseeing the Hitchin 'Union' were four Guardians, two of whom were Quakers, Joshua Ransom and William Lucas. It was the London Commissioners who decreed that the existing Hitchin Workhouse was inadequate, and a new

building (no indoor sanitation, no piped water) to house 240 paupers was approved and opened in 1837 on the north-west outskirts of Hitchin. 'The Union', heavy with deprivation, hardship and stigma, remained a workhouse, even when it came to be known as Chalkdell House, until in 1948 the National Assistance Act repealed all remaining pauper laws. I find it extraordinary to remember that my mother served as a Guardian from the late 1930s, regularly visiting Chalkdell and the Royston Workhouse, appalled by what she saw but deeply impressed by the way that many of the staff were trying to bring some decency and dignity into those settings of great injustice. With its buildings transformed, Chalkdell now has a very different and vital role as Hitchin Hospital as part of the Lister Hospital group, serving as its annexe for the care of the old and chronically sick.

20 In Cowper (William Francis Cowper, Lord Mount-Temple, 1811-1888) and Brand (Henry Robert Brand, Lord Dacre and 2nd Viscount Hampden, 1841-1906) Hertfordshire had Liberal MPs of very different stamp, even though both were aristocrats, inhabiting great estates and both had short army careers in fashionable regiments. Brand served the government in Canada and Australia and represented Hertfordshire from 1868-1874. The *D.N.B.* gives no account of any particular achievement or interest. Cowper's record of public service to his country was outstanding, and his response to the nation's need for social reform, particularly in the fields of education, sanitation and health, was very personal. His approach was that of a philanthropist. He had a special interest in land reform and was instrumental in saving Epping Forest from enclosure in 1871. John Ruskin, a passionate social reformer, was a personal friend, and Cowper was a founder member of his Guild of St George. Hitchin was represented in Parliament by Cowper from 1835-1868.

21 **Lax's Pond:** One of the beauty spots of nearby St Ippolytts, on the estate of a long-dead Professor Lax who lived at St Ibbs. In the drought of 2006, I write this in July, the Pond has again run dry.

22 '**Mount Pleasant**' in William Lucas's diary would have referred to his two fields on the south side of Manly Highway (now Pirton Road). A descendant, William Beck, wrote that Lucas's "fondness for trees and shady groves was especially seen in two places on his own land, one of them being where he had converted an old

and disused gravel pit into a plantation that well deserved the name it acquired of Mount Pleasant." In 1843, on the westerly side of his Manly Highway land, Lucas built Mount Pleasant Cottage which was demolished in the 1930s. For years it was the home of William Dawson, one-time tutor to the Lucas family and a much-loved scholar of high standing in the town, who had been an early pupil of Hitchin's British School, Headmaster of Pirton's British School and librarian of the Mechanics' Institution. As tutor and friend he had the love and respect of young Tukes and Seebohms, and it is worth a visit to Hitchin Cemetery to find and read the verses on his tombstone. In 1843 Lucas wrote "My new gardener, Clark, who resides in the cottage of Mount Pleasant appears an active, hard-working man, though I fear not an accomplished gardener." In 1848, "I am cutting down a considerable extent of the old plantation at Mount Pleasant, digging the ground over and replanting."

One of the fields growing lavender for Perks and Llewellyn (a chemist's shop in Bancroft, still intact in the Hitchin Museum, from which Hitchin lavender products were sent all over the world) was at Mount Pleasant, adjoining the Lucas property. Nearer to the town and separated from the Lucas fields by a brick-walled footpath were the grounds of Mount Pleasant House, a mansion built on the model of Strawberry Hill (and later known as Rosenberg) "in the highest Gothic taste". It was demolished in the 1960s making way for a large residential estate which perpetuates the name of Mount Pleasant, the fine specimen trees saluting those of the great Seebohm and Ransom plantings on the other side of town.

23 **Jordans** has for so long been one of the country's most venerated, loved and visited Meeting Houses, that it is hard to realise that having been started in 1688, after the Declaration of Indulgence (earlier meetings having been held in the great barn of Old Jordans Farm) and having been at the hub of a circle of remarkable Friends, including Penns, Peningtons and Ellwoods, the meeting went into prolonged and sad decline. Minute Books record "as to the prosperity of Truth, things seem to be but lowish in the general...", in 1754 "we have been rather declining of late...", in 1979 "there are now but two ancient men who attend to keep up the Meeting." Regular meetings for worship were discontinued in 1793 and were

not revived until 1926, owing much to the energy of Friends in the recently built and buoyant Jordans Village. But since 1851 some continuity had been kept by the regular holding of a Monthly Meeting in June. A letter to *The Friend* (Seventh Month, 1866) describes vividly how good, comfortable Victorian Friends (add Edwardian, and right on) could combine edification with a jolly good spree. "It is a kind of pic-nic meeting, as the premises are nearly surrounded by beechwoods, and the carriages and horses are placed among the trees, although there is a commodious stable; but this year, I suppose forty horses were retained to convey away all the numerous Friends who attended from London and elsewhere, the Friends of the associated meetings bring provisions for dinner and tea, which are set out on tables improvised on forms without backs... the establishment of Christ's Kingdom was ably set forth" together with "the fulness and freeness of the way of salvation".

24 **Grave:** The word is puzzling in this context. One of the *O.E.D.*'s definitions is "an excavation of any kind. A pit, or trench. Obsolete except in sense of a "trench earthing up potatoes and other roots". Joseph Wright's *Dialect Dictionary* also gives "the winterstore of potatoes, covered, as in a clamp".

25 This was clearly a matter of great importance to Joshua. For 'steady', 'seasoned' Friends of his background, the heart of a Quaker Meeting for Worship was in its focus on the Holy Spirit, 'the Light', 'the Seed', and the prayers were for guidance from within. Friends were very well versed in the Bible for their private use, but the reading of lengthy passages from the scriptures in meeting was, to many, a painful innovation. Older Friends knew only spontaneous, 'given' ministry (though that too could be very lengthy), and many will have found it hard to accept a prepared reading from the printed page.

26 **Wain Wood:** The countryside around Hitchin is rich territory both for naturalists and historians. When Hitchin Quaker families made their excursions and took their walks to Charlton, Preston, Wain Wood, Bendish, Offley, Lilley and the Barton Hills they would have botanized, bird-watched, sketched and chattered, and they must surely have been very much aware of being in Bunyan country. It is the landscape of the *Pilgrim's Progress* and Bunyan was a frequent visitor to Hitchin. In Wain Wood, near

Preston, there is a natural amphitheatre, known now as Bunyan's Dell, and here, at night, there were clandestine gatherings, while look-outs kept watch. Hundreds came to these meetings and their vigour and loyalty is reflected today in Hitchin's thriving Baptist congregations. Because of its age and its continued richness of flora and fauna, Wain Wood is now designated as a Site of Special Scientific Interest.

27 **Anemone banks:** *Anemone Pulsatilla Vulgaris*, Pasque flower, is a beautiful and now rare flower of the chalk downs once growing freely on the Pegsdon Hills outside Hitchin. The local name for it was Danesblood, for tradition maintained that it thrived on old battlefields where the Danes had been defeated. In his *Handbook to Hitchin and the Neighbourhood* (1871) C. Bishop describe the Pasque flower "with its golden cluster of stamens surrounded by a purple blossom of silky texture. This flower is honoured every year by a number of visitors, and therefore, its locality need not be mentioned." Aillie Latchmore, in *People, Places and Past Times of Hitchin* (1974) recalls the picking of the flowers at Easter. They were still unprotected in the 1930s and I can remember the excitement of finding them. It was natural to pick wild flowers then, and I believe my mother planted some roots in the chalky soil of our garden off Letchworth Lane. In 2003, a survey was organised by Plantlife International and the Wild Plant Conservation Society giving every county the chance to choose for an emblem the wild flowers it felt to be most its own, most representative. The Pasque Flower was Hertfordshire's choice

28 **Leeds Infirmary Exhibition:** The 1868 National Exhibition of Works or Art was an extraordinary achievement that deserves to be long remembered. By a brilliant piece of lateral thinking (suggesting not a committee decision but one person's entrepreneurial brain-wave) the empty wards of the new General Infirmary were imagined as a series of natural galleries. Gilbert Scott, in designing the Infirmary, had consulted Florence Nightingale on the plans for the thirty-bed wards; the magnificence of St Pancras Station and the practicality of St Thomas's Hospital were both reflected in Leeds, and the idea of a great exhibition took off. In a few months the building was filled with treasures lent by private collectors, covering not only pictorial but ornamental art in categories as varied as Antiquities,

Metal Work, Carvings in Ivory, Weaponry, Glass, Lace and Embroidery. The opening ceremony was performed by young Edward, Prince of Wales, whose interest in and practical support for hospitals was to be life-long. He spoke of "that liberal munificence which provides at the same time for suffering humanity and for the rational enjoyment of the humblest classes". The Prince's visit was celebrated by a procession, cheers, festivities, music ('Mr Hallé's band' played the Hallelujah Chorus), prayers (from the Bishop of Ripon) and a five guinea luncheon for Subscribers.

29 **Shawe:** The *O.E.D.* gives many instances of 'shaw' or 'shawe' with the meaning of a copse, small wood or a strip of wood forming the border of a field. The word may have some special local significance, explaining 'on the shawe'. There is still a 'shawl plantation' at Leyburn according to the Ordnance Survey map.

30 **Ackworth School** was founded in 1779, largely inspired by Dr John Fothergill, Quaker physician, botanist and philanthropist, in response to the need in the Society of Friends for a school giving a thorough education to the boys and girls of Quaker parents "not in affluence". The impressive school buildings had first been home to the Yorkshire branch of the London Foundling Hospital and from its earliest days Ackworth adopted the idea of the school as 'the family'. When John and Joshua Whiting were scholars in the 1830s they would have lived in a spartan setting with no return home in their three-year stay. They would have been given a thorough schooling to prepare them for an apprenticeship or a trade. It would be hoped, even assumed, that boys would grow up to be hardworking, reliable and scrupulously honest. The records of Ackworth Old Scholars give accounts of many high-achievers in different fields of learning and industry, and many natural leaders, who succeeded, intellectually and materially, far beyond the expectations of their teachers.

31 *The Builder* started publication in 1842, not 'edited' but 'conducted' by George Godwin, F.R.S., F.S.A., who described it as "an illustrated weekly magazine for the architect, engineer, archaeologist, conductor, sanitary reformer and art lover". That sense of scope, not only coupling art and sanitation, but assuming that any competent builder of villas, railway stations and town halls would need to have a sense of the past, led to a truly

remarkable magazine, a great store of Victorian vision and achievement. The front page carried two quotations from Sir Henry Wotton (1568-1639), poet and diplomat: "Well building hath three conditions, commodity, firmness and delight," (*Elements of Architecture*, 1624) and the description of someone's home (from *The Character of a Happy Life*) as "the theatre of their hospitality, the seat of self-fruition, the comfortablest part of their own life."

32 **Gas** came to Hitchin in 1834.

33 **Bee:** A wonderfully appropriate activity for Rebecca and her friends, for as Chambers defines a 'bee' not only as a "four-winged insect that makes honey" but as a "gathering of persons to unite their labour for the benefit of one individual or family, or for some joint amusement, exercise or competition". The latter usage had its origin in the U.S.A.

34 **Grandfather:** This is a reference to Thomas Shillitoe who, in his seventies, spent the years 1826-1829 in the United States.

35 **Mourning Habits:** It may seem strange for a Friend to have bothered to remark on another Friend's wearing of crepe at a time of bereavement. But that noting was entirely in line with the attitude of earlier Quakers whose commitment to their testimony of simplicity often channelled their energies into over-scrupulous observances and harsh words on those who broke them. Though John Whiting would probably have disapproved of any mourning dress as "conformity to the vain and oft-times insincere fashion of the world", it is typical of Joshua that he simply noted facts rather than made comment and we can only guess at his feelings about the matter.

A conventional Victorian funeral, aspired to and achieved by countless families who could ill-afford it, it was an extremely expensive occasion and very public, as an elaborate procession of hearse carriages, outsiders all horses black, all plumed, wound its way. An article in *The Friend* of July 7th, 1866 quotes from the Nonconformist: "there are surely ways enough in which deep and tender feelings can be expressed apart from the raiment which you wear… no need for elaborate pomp and circumstances of woe…" For a widow, 'deep mourning' (if widow's weeds were seriously to be worn) continued for a year and a day, proceeding over months from 'second' to 'third' and then to half-mourning'. The perceived excesses led to lectures on the subject, tracts, pamphlets, letters. 'T.', of *The Friend* described current 'Mourning Habits' as "oppressive bondage", in Queen Victoria's life-time a real airing of the subject, after such mourning as hers, would have been lese-majesty. Common sense needs a long time to come through.

At school in the early 1930s, under a Quaker head-mistress, I can remember that children would occasionally come wearing a black arm-band (a band of another colour warned of a recent vaccination – "don't bump me!"). We took notice of both, and understood without being told that for a while the wearer of the black should be spared from teasing. In a few days the band would be discarded. I do not recall any grown-up commenting on or explaining this relic of 'mourning dress', but I do remember how natural it seemed (and still does) to stand quietly when a hearse and mourners pass.

36 **Langford's men:** The 1862 *Post Office Directory* gives Mrs Charlotte Langford as "cabinet maker, upholsterer, paperhanger and furnishing ironmonger".

37 **Tortoise:** Gilbert White of Selborne inherited a much-loved and closely observed tortoise from his aunt. The 'joyless stupor' in which Timothy (found after his death to have been female) spent so much of his life was noted and deplored by White, but his tortoise's regular awakening at four o'clock in the afternoon makes an appropriate link with Joshua Whiting, for in their absorption in their natural surroundings and in the simplicity of their recordings (given the great difference in their learning and in their backgrounds) the two men had much in common. Another tortoise is known to have had a home in Hitchin and to have been befriended by the banker, scholar and philanthropist, James Hack Tuke.

38 **Ayton School:** The North of England Agricultural School, in the countryside near Middlesbrough, was founded and supported by a group of Quakers (mainly from the families of Pease, Mounsey, Richardson and Backhouse) aware of the needs of children one of whose parents had been disowned for 'marrying out.' It opened in 1841, inspired by the example of Irish Friends, and continued its practical, non-scholastic syllabus, teaching manual rural skills to boys and girls until 1892. It then altered course and served Friends as a regular Quaker school with a full curriculum until it closed in 1997.

# *Bibliography*

There are a great many books, booklets and leaflets brought out by members of the Hitchin Historical Society and by the Society itself. Many of these are listed in the Bibliography or mentioned in the Notes to the Diary and may be found new or second-hand in the well-known antiquarian bookshop of Eric Moore in Bridge Street, or new at Hitchin Museum and Ottakars in the Market Square.

The Quaker Bookshop in Friends House, Euston Road, London, has a strong historical section, and the Library at Friends House welcomes readers and researchers and would give information on the Friends' Historical Society and the Quaker Family History Society. Quaker Meetings often hold material of local interest as well as their specifically Quaker books. The Library at Friends House has been a priceless resource for me. Their multi-volumed *Quaker Dictionary of Biography*, still in typescript, outlines thousands of lives, from the obscure to the eminent, and I should have been lost without it. Old runs of the *British Friend*, *The Friend*, the *Annual Monitor* and the *Friends Quarterly Examiner* were invaluable and fatally absorbing. Above all, I could always count on the knowledge, help and interest of the staff, as indeed I could, and did, in other libraries.

| BECK, William | *Family Fragments* (privately printed) | 1897 |
| BELL, Patricia | *Belief in Bedfordshire* | 1986 |
| BISHOP, C. | *Handbook to Hitchin and the Neighbourhood* | 1875 |

# Bibliography

BRAITHWAITE, Maria *Memorials of Christine Alsop*                  1881

BRAYSHAW, A. Neave *The Quakers: Their Story and Message*          1920

BRIGGS, Asa                *Victorian People*                      1954

                           *Victorian Things*                     1988

BRITTAIN, Vera             *In the Steps of John Bunyan*           1950

BRYANT, G.E. and           *A Quaker Journal* (2 vols)
BAKER, G.P. (eds)          *(William Lucas)*

BURY, Elizabeth and        *Victorian Garden Album*               1992
LEWIS, Philippa

BUTLER, David              *Quaker Meeting Houses*                 1999
                           (Friends Historical Society)

COLEY, Hilda M.            *Our Heritage of Fruits*               1937

DOUGLAS, Priscilla         *Discovering Hitchin*                  1995
and HUMPHRIES, Pauline

FLECK, Alan and             *Old Hitchin*                         1974
Poole, Helen with introduction by Frances Gadd

GLENDENNING, Victoria *A Suppressed Cry*                          1969

GODBER, Joyce              *Friends in Bedfordshire and West*     *1975*
                           *Hertford-shire* (published by Luton &
                           Leighton Monthly Meeting)

                           *History of Bedfordshire*              1969

GRIGGS, F.L.               *An Artist Looks at Hitchin*

# Bibliography

GUTCHEN, Robert M.  *The Government and Misgovernment of Hitchin: 1848-1873*

HERON, Alastair  *Quaker Speak*  2003

HINE, Reginald L.  *The History of Hitchin* (2 vols)  1927-1929

*A Mirror for the Society of Friends* Introduction by Edward Grubb  1930

*Hitchin Worthies*  1932

'Samuel Lucas, His Life and Art-Work' *Walker's Quarterly* no. 27  1928

HUISH, Marcus B.  'Birket Foster, His Life and Work' *Art Annual*  1890

ISICHEI, Elizabeth  *Victorian Quakers*  1970

JAY, Bill  *Victorian Cameraman*  1973

JOHNSON, W. Branch  *Reginald Leslie Hine* (Hertford-shire Past & Present, No 14)  1974

KNIGHTLY, Charles  *The Customs and Ceremonies of Britain*  1986

LOUDON, Jane  *Instruction in Gardening for Ladies*  1840

LATCHMORE, E. Aillie  *People, Places and Past Times of Hitchin*  1974

# Bibliography

LITTLEBOY, Anna          *History of Jordans*                    1934
                         Friends Book Centre

LUCAS,, Francis          *Sketches of Rural Life*                1987
MORGAN, J. and           *The New Book of Apples*               1993

PHYTHIAN, B.A.           *An Encyclopaedia of Dates*            1990

TAYLOR, George M.        *The Little Garden*                    1948

THOMPSON, Henry          *History of Ackworth School*           1879

TUKE, Anthony (ed)       *History of Barclays Bank*             1926

UNDERWOOD, Andrew *Ampthill, A Goodly Heritage*                 1976

VIPONT, Elfrida          *Ackworth School*                      1991